TRAINING COLLEGE STUDENTS IN INFORMATION LITERACY, 2006-07
Edition

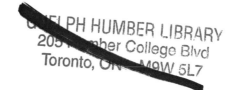
ISBN#: 1-57440-081-9   Copyright 2006   Primary Research Group Inc.

TABLE OF CONTENTS

ABOUT THE AUTHORS & INTERVIEWEES

INTERVIEWEES

Syracuse University is a major research university with highly ranked programs in library and information science. We spoke with Abby Kasowitz-Scheer, Head of Instructional Service at the Syracuse University Library.

The University of Windsor is a Canadian University with more than 16,000 students. Although primarily an undergraduate college, the university also has a well known business school and numerous graduate programs. We spoke with Tamsin Bolton, Information Literacy Librarian at the Leddy Library of the University of Windsor (Ontario, Canada).

The University of North Texas is the flagship college of a subsystem within the public university system of Texas. We interviewed Frances May, Coordinator of User Education and Outreach

The University of North Carolina at Chapel Hill (UNC at Chapel Hill) is one of the Nation's premier public research universities. We spoke with Ms. Lisa Norberg, Coordinator of Instructional Services for the University Library.

Indiana University
We spoke with Carrie Donovan, Instructional Services Librarian, Information Commons, Undergraduate Library Services, Indiana University.

University Of Southern California At Los Angeles Health Sciences complex serves professional programs in occupational therapy, physical therapy, public health, medicine, and pharmacy, as well as some graduate students in the life sciences. We interviewed Russell Smith, Educational Support Librarian, the Norris Medical Library of the Keck School of Medicine at the University of Southern California (USC).

The University of California Berkeley We interviewed Pat Maughan, Project Manger the Mellon Library Faculty Fellowship for Undergraduate Research and Library User Research Coordinator for the Teaching Library of the University of California, Berkeley.

Ulster County Community College, part of the New York state university system (SUNY) has approximately 1900 FTE students. The College devised an innovative information literacy course in 1992, and has been at the forefront of undergraduate information literacy instruction since then. We interviewed Robin Walsh, Coordinator of Information Literacy for the college library.

AUTHORS

Gary R. Fick (gfick@spu.edu) has a Master of Science in Natural Sciences, a Master of Library Science, and a Master of Arts in Biomedical History. He is a Professor of Natural Sciences and Information Literacy Lead Librarian for the Sciences and Psychology at Seattle Pacific University.

:

Anne Pemberton (pembertona@uncw.edu) received her Master's Degree in Information Science from the School of Information Sciences at the University of Tennessee, Knoxville in 2000. She previously served as a North Carolina State University Libraries Fellow and as Social Sciences Librarian at the University of Tennessee, Knoxville before coming to the University of North Carolina Wilmington in 2003. She currently serves as the Instructional Services Coordinator for Randall Library.

Kathryn Batten received her Master's Degree in Library Science from the School of Library and Information Sciences at North Carolina Central University in Durham, North Carolina in 2001. She has worked at the University of North Carolina Wilmington since 1995 and currently directs the Curriculum Materials Center, a satellite branch of Randall Library, and serves as the Education Librarian.

Sharon L. Morrison (smorrison@sosu.edu) is Library Director of the
Henry G. Bennett Memorial Library, Southeastern Oklahoma State University
She has an MLS degree and her work experience includes 20 years public school librarian; 7 years adjunct community college librarian; 3 years reference and instruction librarian; 2 years library director. Publications: Reviewer for *School Library Journal*; forthcoming: "Lawrie Tatum" in *Encyclopedia of Oklahoma History and Culture;* "Chocolate War"; "Radio Act of 1912"*;* "Radio Act of 1927" in *Encyclopedia of the First Amendment.*

Susan S. Webb (swebb@sosu.edu) is collection development director for (580-745-2934) The Henry G. Bennett Memorial Library, Southeastern Oklahoma State University. She holds an MLIS degree and her work experience includes 4 years public school teacher/librarian; 4 years public library director; 8 years technical services librarian. Publications: *Collection Development Curriculum for Oklahoma Public Librarianship Institute;* forthcoming: "Love County" in *Encyclopedia of Oklahoma History and Culture;* "Book Banning"; "Indian Appropriations Act of 1896"; "Blacklists" in *Encyclopedia of the First Amendment.*

Susan Slaga (slagas@ccsu.edu)**is** Assistant Reference Librarian for the Elihu Burritt Library Central Connecticut State University. She has an M.L.I.S. from Simmons College, Boston, MA. Her work experience includes: Assistant Reference Librarian for Central Connecticut State University since 11/2004 as well a reference librarian with the Nashua HH Public Library and Daniel Webster College. Publications/Presentations**:** *Library Instruction in Higher Education* presented at: Connecticut Library Association, Reference & Adult Services Committee conference – 9/2005; *Encyclopedia of American Business* (a Fact on File publication), Management Guru entry Elihu Burritt Library Newsletter.

James Moses has a Masters Degree in economics and public affairs from Columbia University and has written many monographs on information science for Primary Research Group.

INTRODUCTION & SUMMARY OF MAIN FINDINGS

MORE THAN LOVE

Information literacy requirements tend to percolate just beneath the surface of many colleges, and just the right catalyst can send an eruption of information literacy concerns flowing up to the surface. Information literacy is on virtually every college's agenda; it has become a kind of politically correct pursuit and no decent academic – librarian, scientist, administrator or humanist – is unaware of or opposed to better information literacy training. Nonetheless, like many purveyors of good causes, information literacy supporters and, well, activists, can be shortchanged and therefore often feel the need to pursue their interests more aggressively. Information literacy is on the lips of most college administrations but is not always in their wallets.

If there is one common thread in the experiences of twelve colleges profiled in this report, it is that effort is required to see that information literacy acquires salaries and budgets and 'bricks & mortar" as well as merely a good name. The effort requires alliances with higher education administration, departmental chairman, library directors and others. Information literacy must strive to be more than loved, but also housed, fed and clothed; the prospects for this to happen are improving.

The University of Windsor's Tasmin Bolton notes that the University President embraced the concept of information literacy and enshrined it in the University's five year plan. Once this was done, interest in information literacy increased dramatically. The Library had already been highly involved in information literacy through the traditional English composition course and other introductory courses designed mostly for freshmen. However, when the importance of information literacy was literally "put into the constitution" librarians were able to clarify and heighten its role.

A concept is highly esteemed, but perhaps under-funded, can substantially benefit by the simple act of enshrining it as an important issue in official documents.

EXPLAINING LIBRARY EDUCATION

One major impediment to better information literacy is the lack of knowledge that many faculty members have about the library's instructional capabilities and how to use those capabilities into their courses. How to educate faculty members about what the library has to offer was a key theme in many of the profiles and articles in this report. Many libraries have designated specific librarians to deal with particular faculties exclusively on training and information literacy issues. Syracuse University, for example, developed a special program which it dubbed TRAILS, Teaching Research and Information Literacy Skills. Through

Trails, Syracuse information literacy librarians articulate the instructional capabilities of the library and help end users to choose the library instructional services most appropriate and beneficial for them.

ONE CREDIT OR MORE?

Many libraries have had problems with three credit information literacy courses and some have abandoned them in favor of one or two credit courses. In general it is hard to fit three credit courses into a major or turn them into required courses. For three credit courses a big issue is: where does the money come from? It is very expensive adding a three credit course especially if it is a required course. Just think for a moment if any major field wanted to add a university-wide required course that would have to be taken by up to a quarter of all those enrolled, a very ambitious from the point of view of the administration.

The University of North Carolina Wilmington took an interesting approach to the development of a three credit information literacy course by teaming up with the University's computer science department, which wanted a library technology course for a proposed information technology minor. The alliance proved helpful in ultimately winning approval for the course.

Syracuse University offered a 3-credit information literacy course in 2006, and intended the course to be predecessor of, and trial run for, an information literacy course required for graduation. Enrollment was lower than expected and the course may be scaled back to two credits. The State University of New York's Ulster Community College also developed a three credit information literacy course, in 1992, but later decided that only a shorter course could become a college requirement. The University of North Texas plans to offer an information literacy course of two or three credits, but will probably offer it through the University's School of Library Science.

ASSESSMENT

The good news is that library educators are perhaps ahead of the curve in meeting the assessment revolution that is sweeping higher education and will probably grow as pressure increases from state legislatures, for profit higher education, and accrediting agencies etc. Libraries need to be ready for this with assessment info.

Repeatedly, the issue of assessment emerges as perhaps the key issue in information literacy efforts. Librarians at Southeastern Oklahoma State record their journey from a bricks and mortar approach to assessing their library to one aimed at careful assessment of end user capabilities. The frequent use of online quizzes and tutorials and growing use of in-class automated personal response systems have given teachers new assessment tools that are well suited to information literacy training. The availability of standardized data on the information literacy of college students has provided important benchmarking data. Also, as information literacy become more a part of the "normal" for-credit curriculum, the assigning of grades for information literacy courses or components of courses has become more common and the use of pass/fail or non-graded instruction appears to be declining.

SPECIALIZED COURSE IN BLOGS & RSS FEEDS

Short but focused courses on how to use blogs and how to set up RSS feeds and search alerts have become popular recent information literacy topics, particularly for graduate students and faculty. Colleges that stay on top of new developments and deliver short focused and timely courses and seminars increase their prestige within their institutions of higher education. Timing is an important consideration.

INFORMATION LITERACY FOR GRADUATE STUDENTS

Library instructional staffs are increasingly targeting graduate and professional students for information literacy initiatives. In some cases, this has been driven by developments in the academic disciplines themselves. In medicine, the growing influence of evidence-based medicine, which requires facility in the use of medical databases, has been the catalyst. In law, the growing importance of new information technologies in law practices has set off a new round of interest in information literacy.

In some cases, libraries are hiring instructional librarians for the expressed purpose of canvassing, monitoring and providing information literacy services to graduate and professional students and scholars. UNC at Chapel Hill is in the process of hiring a full time librarian to focus on the information literacy requirements of graduate students. The University of North Texas has had great success with highly focused weekend workshops for graduate students, many of them part timers, who have difficulty coming to campus during the week. The USC Health Sciences Library has hired a biologist to teach the use of advanced genetic databases.

The message for most practitioners is that an enterprising sprit here is necessary. Forge an alliance with a sympathetic professor in a field and then identify the information literacy problems in a particular area. Are students or faculty having problems with a particular database? Are the special collections in the field and related fields digitally accessible? Are scholars aware of programs to make them accessible? Do they know what is new? What is available in digital formats and what is not? What can be accessed through the library's e-journal collection and what cannot? How capable are grad students in monitoring blogs or setting up RSS feeds?

USE OF NEW TECHNOLOGIES

Information literacy librarians are using new technologies in reasoned and practical ways, and they hold up promise for better assessment, more student participation, and greater awareness of the full range of information resources.

One exciting area is the growing interest in teaching students and faculty how to use the myriad of special collections often made available on the web, especially by major research libraries. Lisa Norberg of UNC Chapel Hill holds workshops for faculty to help them to incorporate digitized special collections into their teaching. The promise is that as digitized special collections are more increasingly used in the classroom, that their creators will make them more "teacher friendly" a phenomena that is already happening and can be further encouraged by information literacy efforts designed to spur their use.

Wickis are also finding their way into information literacy efforts. The University of Windsor's Bolton is developing an information literacy wicki which can be integrated into subject specific wickis or used stand alone.

Personal response systems that enable instructional librarians to quickly ascertain what students understand or do not understand have proven particularly useful to library educators who often have only very limited time to diagnose and respond to their student's level of comprehension.

Instant message based chat services and virtual reference systems have also shown themselves to be useful, especially in dealing with distance learning students or others who may find it difficult to visit the physical library but who still need to use library databases, often from remote locations.

The most commonly used technology in information literacy is the extensive use of online tutorials. The program *Captivate* seems to be emerging almost as a standard for online information literacy tutorials. Short, highly focused tutorials that focus on highly specific tasks such as how to use a particular database or how to use the library catalog, are the mainstays. Some librarians seem content to use the tutorials developed by other universities, and the collection now available online for use by an interested party, is so extensive that it seems that every library would at least want to consider at least the temporary use of the tutorials of other colleges.

MARKETING AND OUTREACH

Repeatedly, those interviewed for this report expressed the need to reach out to students and faculty, to inject information literacy in small doses within the context of day to day paper writing and class taking. Instructional librarians are like combat nurses, often ignored until needed, but deeply appreciated when they materialize at the right place at the right time.

Indiana University gives its information literacy classes in an information commons area that is a specialized instructional cluster but with many reference librarians and resources ready at hand. This creates a natural flow between instruction and actual use. Berkeley has a grant from the Mellon Foundation to develop a community on the campus devoted to the development of critical research and thinking skills. This community would know how to exploit the library's resources and build information literacy concepts into the curriculum of courses.

REDUCING THE DIGITAL DIVIDE

Many colleges have specialized programs for students from disadvantaged backgrounds to introduce them to scholarship and the kinds of intellectual demands of college life and librarians are playing an increasing role in these programs. Since these programs have evolved into major vehicles for librarians to reach students, more study is needed on the effectiveness of library programs in this area.

HOW FAR ADVANCED ARE SMALLER COLLEGES AND UNIVERSITIES?

Interestingly, many of the smaller colleges and universities such as Seattle Pacific and Ulster County Community College were further along in their information literacy efforts than some of the major research universities. Smaller institutions may feel more pressure to assure that their student bodies are well trained and prepared and may take less for granted than the larger or more celebrated research universities.

It is an interesting and perhaps classic example of the turtle and the hare. The hare (the research university) is confident, perhaps overly so, in the information searching capabilities of its student bodies. The students and the faculty are reluctant to ask for help and reluctant to make information literacy required; they tend to view it as a skill that they should have picked up along the way, or at least as one which they can pick up on their own with little effort. The smaller colleges on the other hand, are more suspect, probably justifiably so, over the information literacy skills of their students, and often strive to make greater efforts to evaluate and educate them.

SYRACUSE UNIVERSITY

Syracuse University, located in Syracuse, New York, is a major private research university with a highly ranked program in library and information science. In 2005, Syracuse had more than 18,000 students of which more than 12,000 were undergraduates. We spoke with Abby Kasowitz-Scheer, Head of Instructional Service at the Syracuse University Library.

Ms. Kasowitz-Scheer heads up a small department whose mission is to coordinate and manage the instructional activities and information literacy initiatives of the University Library. Kasowitz-Scheer has a small staff of one instructional services specialist, and a 0.6 FTE employee who is shared with another section of the library.

INFORMATION LITERACY REQUIREMENTS

Currently, the University does not have specific information literacy requirements for graduation, though some individual specialized programs may have subject specific information literacy requirements. Kasowitz-Scheer feels that the push for information literacy at the University is currently coming largely from the Library, which is making major efforts to overhaul its information literacy procedures. It hopes to convince the University to institute a university wide information literacy graduation requirement. Kasowitz-Scheer also feels that some impetus for change is coming indirectly from accreditation agencies, such as the Middle States Commission on Higher Education, which have emphasized information literacy capabilities in their accreditation reviews.

Kasowitz-Sheer hopes that the building pressure may help win new info literacy requirements but for the time being, much of what the University does in information literacy is the basic work often done in lower level English courses.

"Most of our work currently is with the writing program," says Kasowitx-Scheer, "but we don't have anything formal right now."

ONLINE TUTORIALS

The Library plans to launch its first information literacy tutorials in a few months; they are currently in testing. Kasowitz-Scheer believes it is important to aim your arrows precisely when developing online information literacy tools. Preparing instructors to use the tutorials and other course materials is also sometimes a factor neglected in information literacy tutorial development, she believes. In many ways, the course materials have not just to be beneficial for the students but "sold" to put it a bit crudely, to the instructors. This selling process is sometimes neglected, she believes.

"We have been trying to create online tutorials. My first attempt was to create a major information literacy tutorial but it did not get off the ground and we are trying to do shorter, more focused tutorials. We have also done other web guides for specific courses and specific departments and those have had mixed success. The times where we have created web guides for different courses, they have been for very large courses with many sections, taught by different instructors. For example, we created a web guide for the sophomore writing class – Writing 205 – it is a follow up to the basic Writing 105." Writing 205 is also a required course for most students.

"So we created a web guide to help them along with the research process and we had work sheets and lists of resources for the instructors and we found out that some instructors used it as we intended and some had the students go through it quickly. It wasn't always used as we had intended it to be used."

Kasowitz-Scheer also felt somewhat frustrated by the Library's uneven degrees of access to the students in Writing 205.

"In some classes that use this tutorial the students also came in to the library but we don't see all the students in that program. So we are attempting to reach more students through the web guide and it made some impact but not the impact that we had intended. We did have sessions with the instructors teaching these courses so I think that probably helped some of them understand what we were trying to do."

POLICY ON USE OF TUTORIALS OF OTHER COLLEGES

At first, Kasowitz-Scheer considered using some of the existing tutorials made available by other colleges.

"I looked at TILT (a University of Texas tutorial) and thought about it but we thought it made sense to come up with something home grown that would hook into our resources."

However, like many college libraries, Kasowitz had a shortage of on-staff programming capability. This led to the use of interns from the University's highly regarded School of Library Science.

"The first few interns put together a basic HTML site to take people through the research process, and we had another intern who used *FLASH* and used games and all kinds of interactive activities to reinforce the content and it looked great. But when the intern left there was no one who could develop it. Once that intern left that was it; it as finished.

Our most recent interns have used Macromedia's *Captivate.* It is kind of like an animated *PowerPoint. We* have had the last two interns work on this program and these will be our first official tutorials."

The first tutorial is a general introduction to the Library, and the second is about plagiarism. Kasowitz-Scheer plans to test the plagiarism tutorial this summer through a course at the University's School of Public Communications.

Kasowitz-Scheer would like to develop a suite of tutorials covering different topics, including (but not limited to) use of the library catalog, use of online databases, evaluating sources, and selecting a research topic.

THE TRAILS PROGRAM: TEACHING RESEARCH AND INFORMATION LITERACY SKILLS

In 2005 the library developed the TRAILS program (Teaching Research and Information Skills) to reach out to faculty to explain what the library would offer in terms of helping instructors to incorporate information literacy concepts into their course content. Kasowitz-Scheer explains the program:

"TRAILS was our way of formalizing our instruction program and offering sets of instruction sessions based on different topics. Until last fall we just expected faculty to come to us and make a request and we would fill it and a lot of times they did not really know what they were asking for. There was a lot of confusion on both ends. So we tried to define a little bit better what types of sessions we can offer. We present it as a menu so they can select different types of sessions.

We have broken them (the library's information literacy instructional capabilities) down into five categories:

Introductory
Library Resources and Services
Database Searching
The Research Process
Subject Specific Collections

And these sections in turn are broken down into 21 total sub-sections. We rolled it out in the fall 2005. We are just starting to do assessment right now and we have just sent out a link to a feedback form and reaction has been very positive."

Kasowitz-Scheer strongly feels that faculty often lacked the ability to clearly articulate their needs and to match those needs with the library's instructional capabilities. TRAILS enables the end user to grasp the library's capabilities and diagnose instructional need and match it to the library's capabilities. She felt that the concept was particularly useful to new faculty or others who have not yet built relationships with particular librarians.

Kasowitz-Scheer has just started to evaluate the initiative. "We are sending out an email to everyone who used our services in the past year and we are asking them to comment on the session itself – the activities, the presentation, etc."

MOVING TOWARDS AN INFORMATION-LITERACY GRADUATION REQUIREMENT

The College of Arts & Sciences, and particularly the writing program, is the heaviest user of the library's instructional services, but the library has been promoting a basic information literacy course that it hopes will be required for graduation. Kasowitz-Scheer says that she has learned some lessons along the way.

The library offered a 3-credit information literacy course in 2006, and intended the course to be predecessor of, and trial run for, an information literacy course required for graduation.

"The main goal is to have some kind of required information literacy course for all students so this was a test to see how it would be implemented," says Kasowitz-Scheer.

"We got pretty good feedback but the enrollment was very low, eleven, but we were hoping for 25. I think one of the problems is that it was hard to fit another 3 credit elective course in the schedule so one suggestion was to offer it as a 2 credit course that could match up with *Freshman Forum*. This is a one credit course offered to incoming students and it follows a model through which they have different faculty lead groups of students. It is more learning about the community and the campus and it is about getting students settled on campus in the first semester."

Kasowitz-Scheer also felt that it was important not to try to cover too much in the limited time that instructors had with students. There is some tendency to try to cram in everything and, in the process, lose focus and miss the opportunity to impart a few basic concepts, she believes. As in good writing, less may be better than more.

"I had the students keep a blog and I graded blog entries but it consumed a lot of time to read them all. We did a digital photograph assignment, organizing digital photos on the website. They had to evaluate a few websites according to a set of criteria   The final project was an electronic portfolio. (The next time) I think I might focus more on the main project; it was an InfoGuide, kind of a glorified annotated bibliography project and that was the key to learning about different resources and how to analyze information. I think it might have gotten lost in all the other assignments."

Kasowitz-Scheer also wants to think through the marketing of the course more carefully though she thinks the second time around will be easier. She comments:

"It is difficult to market a course to incoming freshmen so it is really up to advisors but we did put up flyers all over campus and now that we have taught it, and the concept is known, we should have an easier time."

Kasowitz-Scheer says that other questions remain to be resolved. For example, if the course is ultimately adopted as a university wide requirement, staff would probably have to be found to teach it regularly.

"We have to decide how we want to implement this. I taught the first one and another person from the library is teaching it now and we are doing this as part of our regular job duties. If we were to expand it we would have to figure all that out – who would teach it, etc."

ADVICE FOR PEERS

"It is a big job. The biggest key is to assess the needs. That is something that we have not done that well here yet. You can be very effective if on a big campus you can find the one area that really needs it (information literacy help) and really wants to collaborate and then you can advertise by example and go from there. It is very ambitious to take on the whole campus all at once."

UNIVERSITY OF WINDSOR

The University of Windsor is a major Canadian University with more than 16,000 students. Although primarily an undergraduate college, the university also has a well known business school and numerous graduate programs. We spoke with Tamsin Bolton, Information Literacy Librarian at the Leddy Library of the University of Windsor (Ontario, Canada).

INFORMATION LITERACY CONCERNS ASCENDANT

The University President embraced the concept of information literacy and enshrined it in the University's five year plan. Once this was done interest in information literacy increased dramatically. The library had already been highly involved in information literacy through the traditional English composition course and other introductory courses designed mostly for freshmen.

"The first year courses that already exist all have information literacy components that bring the students to a certain level, and then we will build on that from there," says Bolton.

The library set out to help various academic departments to incorporate information literacy concepts into their curriculums. Rather than develop stand alone information literacy courses the goal is to infuse all courses with information literacy concerns.

INFORMATION LITERACY IN THE HISTORY DEPARTMENT

The way that the history specialization is organized at Windsor made it an ideal candidate for one of the first subject specific information literacy programs. Bolton explains the emerging history information literacy program:

"We have a pilot program with the History Department where the library works with the core courses in the second year, third year and fourth year. They are set courses (required courses taught each year). One is a research methods course and so they learn about sources and different types of research in history. The idea is to map the history curriculum with information literacy standards so they would gradually increase their information literacy skills throughout their (college) years. We are trying to do something similar with each department but it is easiest with history since they have core courses that everyone has to take."

SIX SESSIONS AS AN INFORMATION LITERACY APPETIZER

In addition to the extensive work that the library does with the English composition classes, it also is deeply involved in a first year elective course taken by many incoming freshmen. The course gives the library instructional staff another chance, beyond the interventions in English composition, to reach first year students. Bolton explains the class.

"Right now I am involved in a course which is a first year Faculty of Arts and Social Sciences course. It is essentially a transition course only open to first year students. When they come out of high school and go into university there can be a real shock and this course is all about introducing them to different disciplines through a central theme. The theme is the future. We have lecturers who come in from all different disciplines and they talk about the future of their field. We have been able to integrate information literacy into this course. We hope to make this a compulsory course but now it is not – we have a cap (on the number of students in the class).

I am on the design team for this course and we basically set the entire course curriculum week by week. The course is very team oriented; it has 200 students and they are broken out into groups of twenty. Five librarians came in and each one had 4 groups of 40 each. We went in about 4 times and a lot of the students also met outside of class with librarians to get more information."

The students who take this course receive four information literacy sessions with librarians, and these students also take English composition, where they would receive two additional sessions with librarians. Consequently, many Windsor students have as many as six information literacy sessions prior to reaching the required history courses where they will have many more.

TRENDS IN THE LIBRARY TEACHING LOAD

The Instruction Department will soon double in size.

"I am a department of one – I am the only one who is dedicated to information literacy but we are hiring another information literacy librarian in June. There is a core group of about 8 other librarians who do some teaching (the staff does not include graduate students).'

We asked about trends in the teaching work load.

"I have only been here a year and a half but it has gotten much bigger. It is because when information literacy became part of the campus plan the departments began to see it as much more important. So that does make us busier. In the end I see librarians spending less time in classrooms and I see what we do being built right into the courses. Right now what we teach is not reinforced right away. They are not always required to do the research and the students do not always see the link between the library and their core courses."

GET IT IN WRITING

It may seem like a minor point but Bolton stresses the importance of recognizing information literacy as a priority in key documents such as the University Five Year Plan. She explains why this is important:

"When the (University) President's plan was being developed, our library president and the information literacy librarian at that time, they were very insistent on getting the language of information literacy into the campus plan. -- just so that the language would be there. The real issue is that it is not a difficult thing to sell to the faculty -- you don't need to sell it. No faculty member would ever say that information literacy skills are not important but now (with the importance of information literacy codified and spelled out in a key document) we are speaking the same language and on the same path. I can go into a meeting and say ---the president has said that the information literacy skills are necessary to graduate so how can we go about doing that (improving these skills)? So it is very important to the deans to meet the information literacy objectives."

USE OF NEW INSTRUCTIONAL TECHNOLOGIES

The library has two educational labs for group instruction and Bolton would like to re-arrange the layout of the classes to make them somewhat more group work friendly. She would like to eliminate the traditional rows of workstations and replace them with group friendly clusters that foster communication between students. In her view, information literacy instruction thrives in an environment conducive to information sharing and group work.

Bolton is also working on the use of wicki technology to introduce information literacy concepts into very large classes (often 200 to 300 students) that cannot be broken out into more manageable groups for library instruction. Bolton is developing an information literacy wicki that can be integrated into classroom wickis for particular subject matter. She explains the plans:

"I am working on a project through our *Center for Flexible Learning* (the essential equivalent of academic computing in the U.S system) so I have some support there from technicians and we are going to use it in a trial. Instructors are going to be able to add content, and I and other librarians will be able to add content though, at this point, students will not be able to add content. At some point in the future, however, we may allow students in more senior classes to add content. The faculty may eventually use it for assignments, telling students to create an entry to the wicki for xyz. The information literacy component of the wicki has a tutorial area and a discussion board will be integrated into this as well. We are in the process of getting commercial course management software (currently the college uses a home grown system) so something like this will be able to be integrated into Blackboard or WebCT."

ONLINE TUTORIALS

Bolton is a big supporter of Qarbon's *Viewlet Builder* for making online information literacy tutorials.

"I am building some now and taking screen shots. We have a lot of them to show how to handle scenarios, each for different databases – and they are quite easy to make. I could probably make one in about half an hour. In *Java* or *Flash* it takes a long time, and if you've done one on how to search a database and then that database changes its interface, then you have to make it all over again."

Viewlet Builder has a freeware edition, and an educational license for the full edition "costs about $200," says Bolton.

ADVICE TO PEERS

"I just came back from the Wilu Workshop in instruction and library use at Acadia University. It has been going for 35 years and one of the things that come up a lot in terms of information literacy, more so at academic institutions, is the frustration of trying to gain respect of faculty. And my advice is to eliminate the fear of approaching faculty and telling them how things can be better. I have had the opportunity to work with faculty on integrating a lot of information literacy into the curriculum and there is no faculty member that I have worked with who felt that they could not use the help or who did not want the library to get involved. Take the time to talk to the faculty. Don't wait for them to approach you. Faculty rely on the library coming to them because they are not thinking about it otherwise. So it is great for the library to take the initiative to prove what they can do. And if you have a good experience with one faculty member people will start talking about it throughout the institution."

ULSTER COUNTY COMMUNITY COLLEGE

Ulster County Community College, part of the New York state university system (SUNY), has approximately 1900 FTE students. The College devised an innovative information literacy course in 1992, and has been at the forefront of undergraduate information literacy instruction since then. We interviewed Robin Walsh, Coordinator of Information Literacy for the college library.

THE ORIGINS OF LIBRARY 111

The one credit information literacy course given at Ulster County Community College (Library 111) is not an officially required course but, since it is a pre or co-requisite for English 102, a course required for graduation from all degree programs, Library 111 is effectively required for all degree-taking students. Library 111 is also a pre or co-requisite for English 227 (technical writing) which may be substituted for English 102.

The library gives the one credit course in five one hour and fifteen minute sessions or seven fifty minute sessions in the fall, spring or summer. Overall, it offers about 25 sections of the course annually, with enrollment averaging 15-20 per class.

The library has received many inquiries about its information literacy class and has uploaded a *Powerpoint* presentation about the class that can be downloaded from the college website, www.sunyulster.edu.

THE ASSERTIVE LIBRARIAN

According to Walsh the most important factor in winning acceptance for the course was sheer librarian persistence. She explains:

"Basically I tell people that the most important thing in starting the course was having dynamic people working here. The course started back in 1992 and the library director at that time was Larry Burke and he and one of the reference librarians developed a 2-credit information literacy class at that time that was an experimental class. The course that they offered in 1992 was expanded to a three credit elective course in 1993. But they realized at that point that getting a 3 credit elective was fine but a limited number of students would be taking it. They wanted to develop something that could be moved into being a required course and a 3 credit course was not going to fit into any of the degree programs. It was going to be very difficult. Many of the degree programs are already taken up and there are not a lot of electives. Students were not going to make time for it so they felt it was necessary to develop the one credit course. In 1994 they developed it. At that time we had a program to train students in a chemical dependency human services program and this program decided to adopt the Library 111 as a program requirement. They felt that the critical thinking and research skills taught in the course would be good for their program. There was a lot of good word of mouth. It helped us to recruit. But the more sections offered the more difficult it became for librarians on staff to teach it. We did not have enough instructors to teach it so they started training faculty here to teach the course and that is controversial but it has worked out very well for us."

TRAINING FACULTY IN OTHER DISCIPLINES TO TEACH INFORMATION LITERACY

The library has drawn from three primary wells to find instructors for Library 111: librarians at the college, librarians at other institutions, and the college's own faculty in other disciplines, as varied as chemistry to English and everything in-between.

"This is where some libraries (that try to develop information literacy courses) get tripped up," says Walsh. "Since traditionally librarians have taught bibliographic instruction then (college) administrations' often felt we should teach the information literacy courses too. But if the course gets too popular and you offer many sections libraries don't have the staff. In our case we dealt with this problem when the course was officially adopted by the curriculum committee. Once it went through the curriculum committee we were allowed to hire adjunct faculty to teach it. That is one of the walls that other libraries run into – not having enough people on the staff to teach it yet not being allowed to hire adjunct faculty. Now, we have a librarian from Duchess County Community College, and a librarian from Marist College, a curator from the Ulster County Historical Society, as well as a librarian from Kingston High School (as adjuncts)."

While librarians from other local institutions have been a useful addition to the staff that teaches Library 111, Walsh says that involving faculty from other departments of the college has been a very successful strategy.

The library requires all potential instructors of Library 111 to take a training course given by Walsh, who teaches it in five two and a half to three hour sessions. She has trained teachers from the schools departments of English, Communications, Recreation, Nursing and Mathematics, among others.

Currently, the college has 10 adjuncts teaching Library 111, as well as instructors from the other faculties, and librarians from the college library. Overall, the college offers about 20 sections of Library 111 per semester, as well as six sections over the summer. Each section has about 15-20 students, so close to a thousand students may take the one credit class per year.

BECOMING A LIBRARY 111 INSTRUCTOR

The first step in becoming an instructor is to take the actual class. Walsh explains: "What we have had them do is that first they take the course and after they have completed the course the library offers a separate course for teachers. I offer training almost every semester – it depends on how many people are interested. Requiring them to actually take the class weeds out the people who shouldn't be teaching it since a lot of people take it and decide that they don't care for it and they are not gong to teach it. And anyone who refuses to take the course is not allowed to teach it."

We asked Walsh if that included librarians themselves.

"Most of the librarians who are teaching now take the course. I guess with librarians I would have them audit it if it were an issue. The librarian who is teaching this summer took the course and that is how she got interested in it. The library arranges for them to take it with a tuition waiver and then the library offers to those who are still interested a one day a week training class for five weeks here in the library.

Usually I do it 2.5 to 3 hours. Half of it is me talking and half is lab, hands on. In that portion we talk about the teachers point of view, techniques we have used in the past, reading assignments for the students. We talk about plagiarism and developing critical thinking skills. We spend that training time showing them what the library has to offer to the class, what their hand outs look like, different approaches to in class discussions. We show them all the different databases and how they are searched."

Does the typical incoming college student really require five hours of information literacy training rather than the two to three hours common at most colleges? Walsh thinks so.

"Most students are not as computer literate as people think they are; they have a great deal of confidence but not a great deal of skill. We don't want our teachers to be intimidated by students who walk in the classroom and think that they are Bill Gates. We build the instructors confidence. Our students are not as good as finding things as they think they are. Google is a wonderful tool but not the be all and end all for research."

ONLINE AND HYBRID VERSIONS OF LIBRARY 111

The college has developed both a fully online version of Library 111 as well as an online-in-class hybrid. The online course if offered system wide to all colleges in the State University of New York System.

Walsh says that the course has received a great deal of support from faculty who appreciate what it has achieved. The online course was developed by a committee and the "chair of the nursing department was actually one of the people who was on the committee to develop the online course."

The online course was developed in stages and faculty from many departments made contributions. "When the online course was developed the Chair of the Nursing Department was the editor of the online class. We had a number of faculty working on it; the person who did the physical design was the Chair of the Math Department and the Chairman of the English department proofed it for it us so we have had a lot of faculty participation in this."

The online course now accounts for about 30% of overall enrollment in Library 111. Generally, about eight of the twenty Library 111 sections offered in a semester are online courses. To control the instructor's work load, the online courses are limited to only 15 students. "Although that (stricture) has been always under discussion," says Walsh, "since we could get more money if we opened it to more students."

Faculty involvement and faculty trust in the end result has spurred the willingness of faculty to use the course creatively.

"We get a lot of input about assignments from the English Department and the Nursing Department." says Walsh. "The Nursing Department gives an assignment to do research on databases and they are confident that they students will get enough background in the information literacy classes so that they can do the assignments. They ask their students to do more research now- they expect their students to use more library resources."

DEVELOPMENT OF A HYBRID ONLINE/IN-CLASS LIBRARY 111

Walsh found that many of the students taking the online course were not really fully equipped to be working independently. She explains:

"A lot of the students here have full time jobs and when we developed the online course it was for students that have a schedule problem or a distance problem. At the same time we have students who are not too information literate that are taking a course completely online. Being totally online is a problem for them because they may not be too computer literate or they do not work well in isolation. In the hybrid course, students will come to the classroom just on Tuesday. They will do the readings or do the assignments. They will get the social support and will get to ask questions face to face.

On Thursday when they are working on their own they will have had the support of being in the classroom. They have the support that you get from being face to face with their teacher. We are trying this for the first time in the fall."

ADVICE FOR PEERS

"You have to have someone who believes in the course who will meet with faculty on an equal basis – the faculty has to buy in on this. The library can't think this up in the library and keep it in the library. You have to have your faculty buy into it. You need someone like Larry to present it to them and get them to buy in. If it is something quietly devised in the library it won't be accepted. We had the right people to push it. When Patricia Mathes was trying to get someone to buy in on this she would lay in ambush for people, she would study their schedules, and lay in wait and ambush and convince them that this was something that needs to be done. That is what a lot of other programs are lacking those kinds of people who will carry you through."

THE UNIVERSITY OF NORTH TEXAS

The University of North Texas, a public university, is one of the largest universities in Texas; enrollment in 2005 exceeded 32,000 students of which about 25% were in graduate and professional programs. The University is the largest provider of distance education among Texas public universities and offers 93 bachelor's degrees, 111 master's degrees and 50 PHD's. We interviewed Frances May, Coordinator of User Education and Outreach, The University of North Texas Library.

MOVEMENT TOWARDS FORMAL INFORMATION LITERACY CLASSES

Currently, most classroom instruction in information literacy is done at the request of instructors, usually those in the main composition and speech & rhetoric classes for incoming freshmen. Last year, the 2004-05 academic year, the library gave 359 formal classroom sessions, generally lasting about 50 minutes each. Rhetoric and English Composition accounted for more than 80% of total requests. However May believes more instruction is necessary and she soon expects to move towards the creation of an information literacy course, hopefully one that will be a required course.

May says that "We are probably going to be changing to where we at least offer the class unit, probably within the next year or 18 months"

Like many library services instructors, May is frustrated with the limited time she has in composition and rhetoric classes to get across key info literacy concepts. "They need repeated exposure," she says, "And they need to learn about a structure that will let them apply critical thinking tools."

May would also like to go into greater depth in information literacy, going beyond the current basic fare of teaching students to find books and to use the catalog and various databases.

TECHNOLOGY PURCHASES

To accommodate a likely move towards more formalized information literacy classes, the library is in the midst of an expansion of its main special classroom for information literacy initiatives. In the coming summer (2006) the library plans to expand its 26 seat technology center to between 40 to 50 seats. The new workstations will be state of the art with shoebox sized computers and LCD monitors.

TESTING AND ASSESSMENT

The library uses a home grown program for testing and assessment. "It uses the capabilities of NetSupport," explains May, who says that the library LAN (local area network) staff developed the application, working in conjunction with the instructional librarians. Through the *NetSupport* package librarians ask students to find a book and to conduct specific catalog and database searches. The tool is used mostly in the English composition courses, while the library uses a "pen and paper" assessment tool in rhetoric classes. "We want them to be able to recognize the different parts of a citation," says May.

ONLINE TUTORIALS

The library has some basic tutorials on various aspects of library usage and is now working on "adding depth," as May puts it. The library has a very successful tutorial on how to use NetLibrary, the Ebook collection, and it wants to develop other, detailed tutorials that go into some of the databases in greater depth than do the basic tutorials.

STAFFING

Much of the actual teaching is done by librarians drawn from other departments, especially from the reference and information services departments. "It is fairly easy to get people to volunteer," says May. May's department itself has one other librarian in addition to herself, as well as a student assistant. The student assistant position has recently been upgraded and May will get a half time graduate assistant from the College's School of Library Science.

INFORMATION LITERACY FOR GRADUATE STUDENTS

May has been gratified that the grad student information literacy workshops that she offers three times a semester "have been packed." She generally holds them on Saturdays to accommodate the many part time graduate students (many studying education, library science and psychology) who work full or part time during the week.

"We have had a really great response," she says appreciatively. "Some of the topics that have drawn a good response are info on how to use the *Digital Dissertations* database, and how to set up search alerts, which some of the students specially requested. I also do an in depth class on Boolean searching." Among other topics, May discusses how to do brainstorming, and how to construct a search using "and"and "or" constructs. Students also like coverage of *Academic Search Premier* and general periodicals databases. May also stresses information on how to use inter-library loan and other services that the library offers, such as its chat-based reference service which, she believes, is particularly important for graduate students to know about.

The sessions tend to draw more students than the 26-seat library education classroom can easily accommodate, and May believes that the expansion of this classroom should ease congestion.

CHAT SERVICE IN INFORMATION LITERACY

May feels that the college's virtual reference chat service has been an effective information literacy tool. The college has long experience with virtual reference and was the second college nationally to develop the service, according to May. The library uses software provided by Docutech. She notes that it is particularly useful for distance learning students who do not often get the chance to visit the campus librarians.

"Our distance learning students use it a lot and when I do presentations for them I make sure it is covered. Where I get to talk to some of the DL students is that some of the classes have days when they have to be here on campus and I do a session with them for about an hour and this is required."

TOWARDS A FULL CREDIT INFORMATION LITERACY COURSE

The two or three credit information literacy course that May is developing is still a work in progress but she hopes to be able to unveil it within 18 months.

"We should be able to offer it through the School of Library and Information Science; it would be under their wing and it would be an undergrad course. I would really like to do two – one that is basic for freshmen and one that is more advanced for upper classmen. I want it to be a required course but I don't know if that is gong to happen. I think once we have it in place and we can shop what it is doing for the students, then eventually we would like to see it as a required course."

ADVICE FOR PEERS

May stresses marketing. "They (library instructors) need to be ready to publicize what they are doing. They have to repeat what they say and many teachers won't remember something until they need it and that is the way people are (in general). I market any chance I get.
We did a poster session for a distance learning initiative on campus and you make visual what you have available. I did something like "Put a librarian in your online course" and if you can market something with a slogan like that it is going to be a hit. I am a speaker at brown bags for some of the campus organizations. Any chance you get tell teachers and student what you do."

UNIVERSITY OF NORTH CAROLINA AT CHAPEL HILL

DESCRIPTION OF UNC CHAPEL HILL

The University of North Carolina at Chapel Hill (UNC at Chapel Hill) is one of the Nation's premier public research universities. We spoke with Ms. Lisa Norberg, Coordinator of Instructional Services for the University Library. Ms. Norberg directs a small staff composed of one full time professional librarian (in addition to herself) and approximately six graduate students (from the University's School of Library Science) three of whom work 20 hours per week, and three of whom work about 10 hours per week. Another individual reports to the Head of the Undergraduate Library but works closely with the Instructional Services Coordinator's Office to liaison with the English composition program, through which much of the undergraduate information literacy effort is coordinated.

The Office provides outreach and instructional programs to any unit of the various libraries in the university's library system. It supports, organizes and schedules large tours and orientation programs, develops online tutorials and other information literacy educational materials, and educates the broader university community in the instructional capabilities of the library.

DEVELOPMENT OF THE LIBRARY'S INFORMATION LITERACY APPROACH TO ENGLISH COMPOSITION CLASSES

As in many institutions of higher education, the library conducts the main undergraduate information literacy effort through the basic English composition courses generally required of incoming freshmen. UNC Chapel Hill offers three distinct levels of English composition, English 101, 102 and 103. Most incoming students are placed in one of these three levels; a few test out completely and are not required to take basic composition courses. Placement is based on incoming SAT scores. Most incoming freshman start in 102, while some start with 101 or 103. However, the three courses are separate and distinct; they are not different levels of the same course. Students who start in 101 then move on to 102 and ultimately to 103, so some students may take three writing/composition courses and most take at least two.

This may be laudable from the point of view of general American higher education, and advisable given the suspect state of the writing skills of most incoming freshmen to American universities, even the more selective ones. However, it does tend to multiply the number of occasions on which writing instructors may seek the library's participation in information literacy projects, and presents a special challenge for library information literacy professionals.

Norberg comments on the work load: "It (information literacy) is a required part of the English program and it has grown over the years. It used to be one fifty minute session but that was a very imperfect vehicle. So now, at least in theory, the teaching fellows are required to bring their classes once a semester regardless of level and we encourage them to bring them in more often and a lot of them do bring them in far more often."

Just as the three composition courses are distinct courses, the library's information literacy sessions cover different topics in the three levels. In English 102 for example, Norberg notes that the library offers three units or sessions, one each for information resources in the humanities, the sciences and the social sciences. The more basic English 101 course covers library introductory topics encountered in the course of a research project. Norberg explains: "That is also a three unit class. In the units we again try to tailor the instruction to the assignment and we have an online tutorial that we request that they go through before they start. The assignments in 101 are different from 102 in that it is often dependent on what their assignment is and what the research requirements are." The ad hoc nature of this process has an educational advantage in that it ties information literacy projects to practical, at hand subject-related tasks.

In English 103 the information literacy projects for each student eventually focus on topics in a chosen or presumed major field of study. The instruction is also organized around three units.

"In 103 they also have three units – popular culture, public issues and professional communities," says Norberg. "It (the professional communities segment) is designed to begin to introduce the students to academia and how writing differs across different professional communities. It gets more into the scholarly and academic journals and most of the assignments there are in the major that they are interested in pursuing and they look at the journals used in that profession."

For Norberg that is when things get interesting.

"It is a difficult unit to deal with. It is real easy for a first year student to say they want to be a doctor but when you plunk them down in front of a biology journal it can be a little overwhelming both for them and for me," she says.

The classes themselves tend to be held mostly in one of the library's three instructional labs.

APPROACH TO GRADUATE STUDENTS

Prior to 2000 the University had many research method and bibliographic instruction classes in the various graduate programs, and these classes often involved the library instructional staff. However, many of those programs had been eliminated or reduced in the late 1990's, but Norberg says that in recent years interest in instruction in research methods for graduate students and faculty has renewed.

The library has recently decided to hire a full time professional to help meet the instructional and reference needs of graduate students and faculty. We asked Noberg to explain what the library is trying to do with the new position:

"We are looking for someone who can be can go out and not be afraid to meet with faculty, who can assess the need for different programs, who can make the faculty aware of the library capabilities for instruction, and who can plan for workshops."

We asked how the search was progressing and what was the scope of the search. "It was a nationwide search and we have three candidates, one local and two who are coming from out of state." When asked, Norberg said that the person chosen for the position would have to be good at outreach and that he or she would pretty much be marketing his or herself to the graduate school communities. Library tours that are part of the graduate school orientation programs are also helpful, she notes, but the main effort must come from the outreach professional.

"It will take some legwork on the part of this person to go out an ally themselves to the key people in the departments and a lot of our success comes from word of mouth, especially at that level," she says.

ONLINE TUTORIALS

The library has developed more than a dozen online tutorials.

"We have a series of tutorials and this is one area where we do try to customize for different needs but they are built on the same template so it is relatively easy to customize," says Norberg. "We have one basic one for English comp and a few others for this sector and then we have a few that are more geared towards grad students or upper level undergraduates. We worked with our subject specialists on the content and we worked with faculty members and students and we run things by them."

The library has developed specialized tutorials for more than a dozen disciplines, including math research, Latin American studies and biology research, among others. Norberg and her graduate student assistants create the tutorials. "Now we are just beginning to use *Captivate* and are starting to create a series of *Captivate* tutorials. Most of them are very short and specific. How to do a title search? How to use the catalog? Or a particular database? Mostly quick examples of how to do something."

GENERAL STATE OF STUDENT INFO LITERACY

Norberg believes that today's students are relatively facile with basic internet search techniques but need extensive help in evaluating the credibility of sources.

"Instruction has been slow to pick up on how things have shifted," she says. "Students come in with relatively good search skills and they usually they can pick up on how to search databases relatively quickly and they are not afraid of the technologies at all. They are weakest in their evaluation of their information sources and where to go if it is not in Google."

NEW INSTRUCTIONAL TECHNOLOGIES

The library has just introduced a personal response system into its instructional services. Norberg explains the utility of the technology:

"Essentially you can hand out little calculator size gadgets and you can create some interactive quizzing as you go through a presentation. You can test students in an informal and anonymous way and so you can assess where they are. You can give true false and multiple choice questions, and they answer by typing on buttons and you can ask a question and get immediate results. The system costs $1200 but we adopted this because our Physics Department had this technology so we did the same. But there are also some products out there that are free." The University has a site license for the system – *called InterWrite PRS*. The hand held devices are purchased separately at a cost of about $15 each. "We've purchased 30 of them for our computer lab," says Norberg, who notes that the devices are often programmed to track particular individuals but the library elects to use them anonymously in library instruction. Consequently an instructor can get a good idea of how well a class understands a give concept yet avoid the occasional intrusiveness of constant testing.

"We just got them in the spring so we just tried it out with one or two classes and this summer we will do training so that we are comfortable using them," says Norberg. "The company will come and give you one free training session with a representative of the company."

Norberg is also enthusiastic about the University's upcoming purchase of *Harvest Road*, a Learning Objects Depository Software.

"We are interested in trying different approaches to online instruction and making it more interactive and more appealing to younger students who are more accustomed to a little more dynamic environment and we are excited about getting involved in different types of learning objects."

Norberg is particularly interested in encouraging greater use of primary source materials in the classroom.

"Most of what we are working on right how has to do with our digital collections," she says. "We would like to help faculty to integrate primary source materials into the classroom. Some of the learning objects will be directed toward students but we have been doing in depth lectures with faculty in history and literature and interdisciplinary fields like African American studies to find out what barriers exist to using special collections in the classroom and how to overcome those barriers."

What has she discovered?

"Well it varies significantly. Different faculty have very different teaching styles and the library has designed most of our special collections with researchers in mind but they are not very usable from a teaching perspective. So for a researcher to have a 300 page narrative on the web for a researcher is great but it is not very user friendly in terms of introducing it to a classroom. We are trying to chunk down our digital collections into more manageable pieces or elements so that they are more user friendly for faculty.

We do a lot of consultation with faculty and most of that has been one-on-one but we are trying this summer to have a workshop for faculty to introduce for them how to incorporate primary source materials in the classroom – both those that we have commercially purchased and those that we have digitized ourselves. Also we want them to know about how we can digitize things for them for use in their class."

VIRTUAL REFERENCE AND INFORMATION LITERACY

Norberg believes that one of the most important, if somewhat unheralded, information literacy tools has been an instant-message based virtual reference system. The library uses an open source program called *GAIM* which can interface with a large number of IM systems such as those of America Online or Yahoo. Norberg says the program is a very cheap and easy way to get into virtual reference and that it lends itself to information literacy applications. She says it requires virtually no technical expertise. The UNC undergraduate library alone handled 1200 queries in October 2005 through this IM system. The library also maintains commercial virtual reference service but she says that the instant messaging service is very very popular and "a very active learning environment. And another similar open source product is called *Trillion*," says Norberg.

ADVICE FOR PEERS

"One big element that is missing in a lot of instruction is usability. I think that Stanley Wilder in his *Chronicle* article made an excellent point: a lot of what information literacy has been about has been teaching students how to get around bad interfaces. I think it is important for instructional librarians to be involved in interface design."

INDIANA UNIVERSITY, BLOOMINGTON

DESCRIPTION OF INDIANA UNIVERSITY, BLOOMINGTON

Indiana University enrolled nearly 38,000 students in 2005, more than 29,000 of whom were undergraduates. More than 7,000 faculty and staff, and 97 librarians serve one of the Nation's best known public research universities. We spoke with Carrie Donovan, Instructional Services Librarian, Information Commons, Undergraduate Library Services, Indiana University.

INSTRUCTION IN THE INFORMATION COMMONS

The undergraduate library at Indiana University holds its undergraduate information literacy classes in the library's Information Commons, a huge open area taking up much of two floors of the undergraduate library. Donovan describes the Commons as: "A hybrid environment that encompasses research and print reference materials and multimedia technologies, pc's and macs. There are three hundred pc's in this area, and the first floor is open 24 hours per day, 7 days per week."

In this vast information services park the library has placed three "instruction clusters" which, according to Donovan "are areas set aside with 25-30 pc's and SMARTboards for the instructors."

The arrangement enables students to use the "instructional clusters" for their own purposes when they are not being used for instruction, a definite advantage at a campus that had 7,000 (seven thousand) incoming freshmen in the current academic year.

"Most info literacy courses are given there," says Donovan, who also points out, "We do have 16 libraries on our campus and a lot of the branch libraries have instructional spaces in their own setting."

Donovan likes the synergies that instruction in the Commons fosters. Students that receive instruction also have a cluster of information experts very much at hand.

"Most of the instruction that we do happens here in the clusters and our reference desk is here as well and they are staffed with one librarian, and one graduate student. The grad students are often technology experts hired by the Departments of Information Resources and Computing on our campus and they handle all questions relating to software, hardware etc."

INFORMATION LITERACY REQUIREMENTS

The University does not have specific information literacy requirements and most of the undergraduate instruction takes place through the basic English composition and Rhetoric/Communications classes for incoming freshmen.

At Indiana, individual instructors have a great deal of leeway in how they organize and teach the basic writing and rhetoric classes, and Donovan stresses the importance of personal relationships with these instructors.

"We do have great relationships with the program coordinators and those courses are mostly taught by graduate students so there is a lot of changeover with the people who teach those classes. We try to go to their orientations and we talk about the library's role particularly in the first year.

Each instructor can say to their students: 'these are the parameters of the assignment for my class' and the instructional librarians have to tailor the instruction for the different classes. When the instructors request a session we have them fill out an online form and we ask them to select from several learning goals in terms of what they want their students to take away from the session."

The library simply does not get too many chances to meet students and instructors and so it is important to get highly accurate needs assessments. The online tool helps the library's instructors to emphasize the right topics and to take the right approach in the limited time that they have."

REDUCING THE DIGITAL DIVIDE

In addition to the extensive work done with the English Composition and Speech/Rhetoric classes, Donovan works closely with the Student Academic Center, which offers basic study skill courses to students who need to improve their basic study habits. "Some students have not had that many research-based assignments and we talk to them about what their professors might expect them to know and what it means to them. We talk to them about the world of information and how to approach it and how to succeed in a scholarly environment."

Donovan believes that sometimes basic introductions to major student tools can jump start a student. "We have introduced many to the Ebsco database *Academic Search Premier*," says Donovan., giving an example.

DEVELOPMENTS IN THE CAMPUS BRANCH LIBRARIES

Donovan says that though there are no formal information literacy requirements on the undergraduate level, there is a great deal of activity within particular disciplines to develop formal subject specific information literacy classes.

She elaborates: "For example a librarian in the life sciences has developed a credit bearing information literacy course for students. It is a one credit course that will be offered as a pilot in the fall and he actually collaborated with several faculty members in the Department of Biology to identify gaps in their students' knowledge relating to biology and how they relate to information. The course is going to lead students through understanding scientific literature and how scientists communicate and also how to read that kind of literature. It is a very focused approach to information literacy and that is one reason why it will succeed."

NEW TECHNOLOGIES

"We are looking into purchasing some classroom control software. We would not use it to control student pc's but to create more of an open learning environment. You can take what is happening on one student's pc and project it to all students. It facilitates understanding and dialog among the students; sometimes one student does a certain search and goes through an explanation (for the other students) but when we have this software we will be able to share it with everyone (on a screen)." Donovan has not chosen a commercial product yet but is leaning towards a product called *Synchoneyes*, and is also considering one called *LanSchool*. She advises all contemplating the purchase of such products to look up a recent major discussion of them on the ILI Listserv, which is hosted by the ACRL.

The Library has also recently purchased a classroom response system.

"Our campus has an agreement with eInstruction," says Donovan, "and there are several instructors on campus who use clickers so we thought that students would be familiar with them. I have used them only in a few sessions and they have been really fun and they help me quite a bit in several ways. They do keep the students really engaged. I intersperse little checking in questions throughout my class. So they understand that there will be a question coming up and they tend to pay a little more attention. But it is nice since the responses are anonymous. This is nice since the resources here at the library are very new to the students. When the results pop up for the question, some of them may think: 'Oh, four other people got that wrong so it is OK for me to ask a question.' It helps me to get feedback right away so I can see whether I am getting through to them or do I need to take a different approach? And this is important since we will only see them one or two times and so you are teaching to them in a vacuum and you can know how effective you teaching is that DAY. I don't use them for every session since they do take a little bit of time. Every time you ask a question it stimulates discussion and can take you off on a different topic."

Are they popular with the students themselves, we asked?

"One time at the end of a class I posed the question: what do you think of the clickers? And 75% of the class said that they enjoyed the opportunity to respond."

EFFECTIVENESS OF GRADUATE STUDENT ASSISTANCE

Donovan believes that the teaching staff's effectiveness is dramatically boosted by the use of a cadre of graduate students. She comments: "The burn out rate is not as high as at other places and one reason is that we do employ 10-12 instruction assistants who are students from our School of Library and Information Science who are interested in teaching. We hire them for a minimum of one academic year and we do ask for a commitment from these students since it takes a lot of time to train them. We call them IA's."

We asked about the cost to the library.

"They get only $7.50 per hour and they are paid only for teaching and not preparing for sessions," said Donovan somewhat apologetically. "A lot of them are taking advantage of this opportunity to get the experience and if you are looking for a job in an academic library a majority of those jobs are going to ask for instructional experience. So it is great for us and every year we have grad students teaching with us who are energetic and they have new ideas and they want to learn as much as they can I think that is one thing that really helps us and also makes it fun and I supervise these students."

The student instructors receive a 4-8 hours training session, augmented by monthly meetings with Donovan, and ad hoc meetings when needed "The training is sort of ongoing and ad hoc and some of our IA's have teaching experience and some have never been in front of a classroom."

ADVICE FOR PEERS

"One thing that I think is so important for us to remember is that academic libraries have taken the role of pushing this forward. It is not necessarily a library issues but all educators should be thinking about this. So we should always be thinking how can we be partnering to build information literacy into what they do. We work with the Admissions Department, we work with athletes. Now we are working on a website that is specifically geared to (the information literacy needs of) student athletes. They travel so much and are away from campus so often. We met with some people from the Athletics Department and we asked them – 'What do you need?' And they told us.

You need to get these conversations going especially with the people for whom it is not so obvious – that would be my advice. Seek out those partnerships; talk to people out there; find out what their students need. Think of the library's role as a great contributor to student learning. That is what we do and we have to embrace it."

THE UNIVERSITY OF SOUTHERN CALIFORNIA AT LOS ANGELES (USC)

DESCRIPTION OF USC AND THE USC HEALTH SCIENCES COMPLEX

The University of Southern California at Los Angeles (USC) is one of the nation's largest private research universities, with more than 33,000 total students in 2005, of which close to half were enrolled in graduate and professional programs.

The Health Sciences complex of the University of Southern California at Los Angeles serves professional programs in occupational therapy, physical therapy, public health, medicine, and pharmacy, as well as some graduate students in the life sciences. The professional programs served by the school have a combined total enrollment of more than 2200 students.

We interviewed Russell Smith, Educational Support Librarian, the Norris Medical Library of the Keck School of Medicine at the University of Southern California (USC).

The crux of the library's information literacy initiative is a program to meet information literacy requirement formulated by the various health sciences disciplines, particularly the School of Medicine. In 1999, the American Association of Medical Colleges developed information literacy requirements which became the basis of the school's efforts.

After an initial orientation lecture, medical students must meet three information literacy standards in areas such as use of *Medline*, and demonstration of ability to search evidence based medicine resources. Students can meet the criteria essentially through self study and the submission of projects that demonstrate the required expertise. Students generally submit their search strategies and the references they pull up during the research, and submit the results to the instructional librarians for evaluation.

"They are given a hands-on lecture and then after that it is pretty much up to them," says Smith.

In addition to this basic form of information literacy testing, the library also conducts many workshops, particularly in productivity enhancing software such as *EndNote* and *PowerPoint*. Although Smith does some of the teaching his efforts are complemented by a broad array of specialists drawn from different areas of the library. The library webmaster, for example, teaches a class in *Dreamweaver*. In addition, the library has recently hired an academic biologist to be part of the library staff, head a new bio-informatics unit, and teach courses in how to use some of the more arcane biological databases, such as *Sequence Analysis* and *Vector NTI*.

TUTORIALS

Smith says that the library's own tutorials are just static web pages and are "nothing to write home about" and he says he is mostly content borrowing other college's tutorials.

"Our tutorials page is really mostly a pointer to other peoples tutorials," he explains, "Duke, for example, has an excellent one on evidence based medicine."

The library does have some new and original things in the works.

"We are working on this program called Tipsheets; basically it will be a collection of one or two page documents explaining things like how to cite online resources, how to develop a database, searching *Chemical Abstracts*, using *PubMed*, working with images, etc. The whole library is participating in that effort and we plan to have at least three dozen of them."

UNIVERSITY OF CALIFORNIA, BERKELEY

BASIC DESCRIPTION OF THE UNIVERSITY OF CALIFORNIA, BERKELEY

The University of California at Berkeley is the flagship research university of the California state university system. In 2005 enrollment was approximately 23,500 undergraduate students and more than 10,000 graduate students. We interviewed Pat Maughan, Project Manger the Mellon Library Faculty Fellowship for Undergraduate Research and Library User Research Coordinator for the Teaching Library of the University of California, Berkeley.

THE TEACHING LIBRARY

The library's instructional division, referred to as The Teaching Library, has 12 full time staff, of which ten have MLS degrees (two others are higher level library assistants). To a greater extent than many other research universities, Berkeley stresses information literacy and, although it has no formal college wide information literacy requirements, its 12 instructors were called upon to give more than 1,334 sessions with a total attendance of 27,764 students in the academic period between Jan. 2005 and June 2006.

Maughan believes in aggressive outreach, and the Teaching Library has extensive ongoing programs with the departments of English, History, Ethnic Studies, Rhetoric and Interdisciplinary Studies, among others. The Teaching Library focuses largely, though not exclusively, on undergraduate information literacy efforts.

INTEGRATED INSTRUCTION

In addition to teaching responsibilities each staff member of The Teaching Library also is designated as a contact person for various campus programs. Maughan, for example, is the liaison for the Academic Achievement Program. This is a program for students that may be somewhat less prepared initially for college life than the norm for incoming Berkeley students.

The Academic Achievement Program, and other specialized programs for students from lower income or other disadvantaged backgrounds, such as the Miller Scholar's Program, and the McNair Scholar's program, form another important target group for The Teaching Library.

"In my case I do 5 sessions for just the group that I am responsible for and those are two hour sessions," says Maughan.

Maughan says that the library is continually looking for new opportunities for its instructional expertise.

"I should say that our campus is extremely diffuse so we don't have campus wide coordination for many things," says Maughan, echoing a tale told on many major research university campuses. "So one of the challenges for us is to identify the existence of programs and partners with whom the library can work and as we find out about them we take steps to introduce ourselves and encourage them to make use of us."

Indeed, the Teaching Library considers outreach so important that is has assigned one person the more or less full time job of contacting instructors and programs on a regular basis to make sure that they are aware of the services that the Teaching Library offers. The unit sends out an email to all departmental contacts each semester, and agitates through library website. "But the most powerful marketing is by word of mouth," she says.

TEACHING LABORATORY

The library has three instruction rooms in its main building and a fourth in an adjoining building. "Our focus is on hands-on instruction," says Maughan and the rooms are equipped with workstations and SMARTboards."

THE MELLON PROGRAM

The library won a major grant from the Mellon Foundation to examine the effects of inserting library instructional personnel into the University's course development process, to see if information literacy concepts could actually be built into the courses themselves.

"The history of library instruction on our campus is more or less at the point of time when the faculty member contacts the library, and that is long after the syllabus has been decided," explains Maughan. "The Mellon program makes an attempt to intervene earlier in the process and we have 12-14 Mellon fellows at Berkeley – in various fields. During their time here they are exposed to a variety of topics dealing with syllabus design, the use of technologies in the classroom, the integration of library research skills into the assignments, and are given an overview of the library resources that are available. Each fellow for the year of their fellowship are assigned an implementation team made up of a campus librarian, someone from Educational Technology Services, and from the Graduate Student Instructor Training Center and, in some cases, they will also be assigned an assessment coordinator (a library staff member).

The idea is that these fellows receive a lot of intensive training and support which allows the library to the reach the goals of the program, which are:

1) To create a community (librarians, students, instructors, technologists, etc) on the campus that is devoted to developing research and critical thinking skills.

2) To focus on developing information literacy skills among large enrollment, lower division courses. "We hope to have a greater impact across the campus if we focus on these courses (many of which have no information literacy component currently but reach a large number of students). One such class, a basic chemistry class, has more than 1200 students," explains Maughan.

The $749,000 project funded by the grant will take place over a 5 year period. The Library's project partners include the Division Of Undergraduate Education, The Graduate Student Instructor Teaching and Resource Center, The Office of Educational Development (a group that does faculty development around teaching), Educational Technology Services (classroom technology), and the American Cultures Program (which offers the one university-wide required course).

Further details of the project can be gleaned from www.lib.berkeley.edu/MellonInstitute.html.

LESSONS LEARNED

Maughan does not underestimate the difficulty of creating a more information literate teaching environment.

"I think if the objective is to reconceive the role of the library as a center of learning through research based teaching approaches, then the library has to work towards building a larger community on campus. This community includes the grad students, the educational technologists, the Division of Undergraduate Education, and the faculty development staff. I think we have been very successful in that. But, having said that, our campus culture is one of decentralization and a lot of individual latitude and freedoms and it is hard to try to achieve a campus wide goal when the centers for implementing that goal are disbursed across the campus. So it is dependent upon the good will and interest of a range of individuals and it can be tough to keep that going. I would presume if the culture is more centralized it may be easier to pull off a program like this than at an institution such as our own."

PART TWO: CONTRIBUTED ARTICLES

INFORMATION LITERACY AT SEATTLE PACIFIC UNIVERSITY: SCALING THE HEIGHTS

By Gary R. Fick

Building an information literacy program is not unlike mountain climbing. Both require conviction, planning, expertise, stamina, and continual evaluation. Both are arduous tasks with challenges and set-backs, yet have moments of exhilaration and success. In short, teaching information literacy is hard work, but well-worth the effort.

INTRODUCTION AND HISTORY

Seattle Pacific University (SPU) is a small, private, comprehensive institution with 3,000 undergraduate and 900 graduate students. We have an undergraduate liberal arts program as well as emphases in education, nursing, business, and theology. At the graduate level we offer a variety of master's programs and three doctoral degrees. The campus has one main library; SPU is located in Seattle, Washington.

Before 1999 library education sessions were given by four liaison librarians primarily when requested by faculty. However, our involvement in the planning of a new undergraduate general education program provided the impetus to re-evaluate the situation. With a foothold in this new common curriculum established, we developed a vision statement and a competencies rubric based off the ACRL information literacy standards as guides to transform ad hoc library instruction offerings into an information literacy program. Succinctly put, information literacy is an understanding of the structure of the information world and applying information seeking skills successfully. The competencies rubric outlines the various ways this definition is actualized.

OBJECTIVES AND PRACTICES

The main long-term objective of the program is to incorporate information literacy at strategic points within each curriculum in collaboration with faculty so that it becomes an integral part of the students' education. Each curriculum has its own structure and requirements, with different information needs, so we use a variety of approaches tailored to particular subject areas. For some curricula, class presentations in key required courses becomes the primary way to focus information literacy. For other programs, guides and pathfinders are posted for their courses on the internet for use with specific class assignments. And, in a few majors with limited enrollments, small group or individual tutorial instruction is provided by a liaison librarian.

We do not offer library information literacy courses for pedagogical and practical reasons. Our past experience in offering such courses revealed that most students did not take them seriously, considering the class irrelevant, usually because it was not linked to a subject area. We also do not have the staff time to devote to this level of class preparation and student contact because liaisons have a variety of other responsibilities.

Currently six liaison librarians, including one who oversees the program, initiate contact and work closely with faculty in finding ways to develop information literacy skills by meeting and planning with individual faculty and curriculum committees. For the common curriculum students, three required online library modules and accompanying ten-point multiple choice quizzes are taken by freshmen and graded during their first quarter of study in the University Seminar (USEM) class. There are thirty sections to this class, each on a different subject. The three modules walk students through ways (1) to use the online catalog and find materials in the library, (2) to manipulate an entry-level periodical database (*Academic Search Premier*), and (3) to use web browsers, particularly Google, effectively, as well as evaluate web pages for academic use.

However, the modules are designed merely to allow students to become familiar with these research tools. Each USEM instructor requires additional subject specific course assignments to reinforce the use of library resources. Typical assignments include short answer exercises, research papers, and/or oral reports. The librarians provide a workshop each year to teach new USEM instructors how to create effective library assignments, as well as familiarize them with the design and purpose of the library modules.

Overall, this introduction to the library provides a standardized starting point for undergraduates. A pre-test was administered to all USEM students in the fall of 2003 and the scores were compared later with the online quiz scores taken at the end of the quarter. On average, the scores doubled from 4 to 8 correct answers per quiz, implying that student learning is occurring. We also used the data to refine quiz questions. Currently feedback elicited from students and USEM instructors is being reviewed to determine how best to upgrade the modules.

The information literacy program continues to grow as more curricula become involved. In 2001/02 75 instructional sessions to some 2000 students were offered by librarians in coordination with faculty. In 2004/05 120 sessions were given to 3300 students. Typically there are 15-40 students per session, with each session usually involving one to two hours of class time. Each session is focused around a course assignment designed to make use of information resources. These are usually held in our library instructional lab where, as an integral part of the class, students practice using the print and online materials presented.

ASSESSMENT

Assessment of information literacy is beginning to occur at three levels. First, there are a variety of approaches used when teaching specific courses. Most often we elicit feedback from students and the instructor after a session, asking what was new information, what was already known, and what could be added or changed. We also review students' research paper bibliographies, and in some cases, librarians grade bibliographies according to specific criteria previously established with course instructors. For a few classes, students identify the process by which they used specific resources and located references so we can find out student practices. Second, library liaisons meet with instructors and/or the curriculum committee to review and evaluate how information literacy is integrated into a particular program. Information literacy elements are examined in relation to program goals and outcomes.

Finally, in 2004/05 we participated in phase III testing of SAILS, the online Standardized Assessment of Information Literacy Skills. From 22 discipline-based capstone courses 324 SPU juniors and seniors (along with over 27,000 university and college students throughout the United States and Canada) responded to the 200 multiple choice test questions. Our students performed slightly above average on the various skills sets analyzed. Further analysis of the data will help us determine how students within particular majors performed, and how well they did on particular questions. It will also help us to decide whether this measure, once finalized, is something to use periodically to evaluate the overall effectiveness of our information literacy program across campus.

SUCCESSES AND CHALLENGES

Moving towards a comprehensive program whereby information literacy is introduced, regularized, and evaluated in each curriculum is an ambitious goal, and we have a long climb ahead of us. While we have gained footholds in many curricula, there is much work to do to fully integrate and evaluate information literacy within these disciplines. For other curricula within such fields as nursing, education, psychology and biology, we have successfully collaborated with faculty to develop critical elements of instruction and evaluation. For these disciplines, information literacy has become regularized into appropriate courses at various stages of the curriculum, including a distance education online Master's degree in education, and various undergraduate and graduate offerings on campus. We also have recently received a grant to equip our instructional spaces with personal response system technology whereby an instructor can ask a question and students, using a hand-held device, can respond. We anticipate developing ways to integrate this approach into our information literacy sessions.

Much of the initial work in setting up information literacy revolves around building relationships with key faculty in the discipline. Collaborating with them to identify and develop curricular junctions where information literacy should occur is critical and takes time. Sometimes changes in library or faculty personnel hamper this process, and sometimes other library objectives take priority. Over the last couple of years we have had changes in liaison and leadership personnel, and have had to pay attention to other projects. And, in a few instances, we have had to take a step back as changes within disciplines have reduced some information literacy components. All of these factors have slowed our progress in moving up the mountain of information literacy programming, so our challenge now is to re-invigorate the campus around this initiative.

To do this we must first re-evaluate where we are and the different routes open to us so we can proceed. To do so also means broadening this conversation to include other key voices on-campus. We have had strong administrative support for developing information literacy, especially when we started out during the initiation of the undergraduate common curriculum. Working with academic administration now is crucial in re-establishing program objectives and directions, and further involving faculty in this process will be another important step. We look forward to all of their support, advice, and collaboration as we move farther along in our continued pursuit of offering information literacy across the curriculum.

CREATING A THREE CREDIT HOUR INFORMATION LITERACY COURSE: ONE LIBRARY'S EXPERIENCE

Anne Pemberton, Instructional Services Coordinator*
Kathryn Batten, Education Librarian
William Madison Randall Library
University of North Carolina Wilmington

*Contact primary author with questions: pembertona@uncw.edu | 910-962-7810

Creating a three credit hour information literacy course at the University of North Carolina Wilmington has been both challenging and rewarding. Libraries looking to establish information literacy courses for credit may find useful the following narrative about the process undertaken by librarians at Randall Library to develop LIB 103.

DIMENSIONS OF LIBRARY INSTRUCTION AT NC STATE WILMINGTON

The University of North Carolina Wilmington (UNCW) has 11,653 students and offers 73 bachelor's degrees, 23 master's degrees, and one doctoral program. The University employs just over 800 faculty members (both full and part time). The library that supports the campus (Randall Library) employs 19 librarians. Eight of the nineteen librarians, referred to as "primary contact librarians," are responsible for delivering library instruction. The library instruction program reached over 8000 students in the last academic year (2004 – 2005) through various instruction sessions such as course-related instruction, drop-in clinics, and library workshops. Currently, the university does not have an information literacy requirement. Therefore, library instruction may be delivered to some departments which actively request instruction but not delivered to those that may not view library instruction as an important component of the curriculum.

INITIAL EFFORTS AT STAND ALONE INFORMATION LITERACY COURSES

UNCW librarians realized the need for another method to deliver library instruction and in 1997 were able to establish in two 1 credit hour courses entitled, *Library Literacy* and *The Electronic Library*. These courses were offered under the umbrella of "University Studies" but were taught solely by librarians. Because these courses had a "UNI" course prefix, they were not visible as "library courses" and enrollment was low. These "UNI" courses were modified over time and several librarians served as instructors. The course names and descriptions were listed initially in the 1997 undergraduate catalog as:

UNI 102. Library Literacy (1) Concepts and methodology for developing library search strategies; locating, selecting, and evaluating relevant information resources. One lecture hour per week.

UNI 103. The Electronic Library (1) Concepts and methodology of electronic information resources. Government and commercial CD-ROM databases, remote databases and Internet resources.

COLLABORATION WITH THE COMPUTER SCIENCE DEPARTMENT

Between 1997 and 2004, no other courses relating to information literacy were established. During the spring semester of 2004, the Department of Computer Science at UNCW approached the library about creating and developing a course for a soon to be established information technology minor. Computer science faculty met with interested librarians to discuss the possibility. Librarians were eager to develop a course and knew that partnering with an academic department would give the course a market, establish credibility for it, and create an opportunity for librarians to offer a new information literacy course. The computer science faculty members were looking for a course on library technology that would complement computer science courses to create a well rounded information technology minor. The structure of the proposed information technology minor required that the library course be three credit hours. Librarians agreed to create, develop, and teach the three credit hour course. After discussions about possible course content, the computer science faculty decided to make the library course a requirement for completion of the proposed information technology minor.

Several questions arose: Which librarian(s) would teach this course? What would be the content of the course? How many sections would be offered? Would the course be offered under "UNI" as were other library courses or would it be offered under the computer science prefix? If the course were offered under the computer science prefix, would the Department of Computer Science pay librarians to teach "their" course? Should the library establish a course prefix of its own? What was the procedure for adding a new course? What methods would be used to advertise and promote the course?

THE POLITICS OF ADOPTING A LIBRARY COURSE PREFIX

Librarians felt strongly that a course prefix strictly for library courses should be established. This would enable the library to control the course content and allow for additional courses to be added in the future. Librarians felt this would be a crucial first step in a long-term goal of establishing information literacy courses that may, at some point, be required on campus. Offering courses under a library prefix, such as "LIB," would give courses more visibility to students as well. It was decided that the library would attempt to acquire a course prefix of

"LIB" for all library courses including the proposed course required for the information technology minor.

Library Pay and Reimbursement Issues for Information Literacy Courses

It should be noted that librarians were warned by the library administration that a salary increase or "overload pay" would not be given if courses were taught under a library prefix despite the added responsibility. Teaching LIB classes would be considered part of regular instruction and would not be considered "overload." Although this was a slight deterrent, librarians still felt strongly that it was important to have a library prefix to maintain control over course content. The first step was to approach the University Curriculum Committee with a proposal for both establishing the course prefix (LIB) and the three credit hour course. At UNCW, the University Curriculum Committee is a University Faculty Senate committee. It is responsible for reviewing all proposals for curricular changes for the campus. The committee submits proposals, along with the committee's recommendations, to the Senate for consideration.

DIALOG WITH THE UNIVERSITY CIRRICULUM COMMITTEE

Fortunately, the Instructional Services Coordinator for the library was an ex-officio member of the University Curriculum Committee and was familiar with the process departments needed to follow in order to create a new course prefix and a new course. In collaboration with the Associate University Librarian for Public Services, the Instructional Services Coordinator filled out the necessary forms and the proposals were placed on the agenda for one of the curriculum committee meetings during the fall semester of 2004. Initially, only the Instructional Services Coordinator attended the curriculum committee meeting to discuss the proposed LIB prefix and the new course. In hindsight, this may have been ineffective. Having library administrators at this initial meeting may have provided stronger support for both the acquisition of the prefix and the creation of the course. Members of the curriculum committee had several questions about the proposals. Admittedly overwhelmed and unprepared for the number of questions asked by the committee, the Instructional Services Coordinator asked that she be given time to consult with the Associate University Librarian for Public Services and report back to the committee at the next meeting. In order to appropriately and effectively address the curriculum committee's questions and concerns, the Instructional Services Coordinator and the Associate University Librarian for Public Services drafted responses and delivered answers in both print and in person to the curriculum committee at their next meeting.

The committee's questions and the library's responses are listed below. These are the specific answers given to the committee. Libraries wishing to establish courses for college credit or wishing to create their own course prefix may find these questions and justifications helpful as their university committees may pose similar questions.

Question posed by curriculum committee: "What is the process of Curricular Formation within the Library?"

Library's response: "Currently, all instruction discussions occur within our Library Instruction Team (also referred to as the Primary Contact Librarian Team). We offer various instruction including UNI 103, course-related instruction, one-on-one instruction, drop-in clinics, tours, etc. This group meets bi-weekly and instruction related discussions are held at this meeting. The Associate University Librarian for Public Services has now formally created a subset of this group to serve as the library's Curriculum Committee. All discussions and processes regarding courses or potential courses with the LIB prefix will go through this committee. This committee will model its procedures after other departmental/college curriculum committees."

Question posed by curriculum committee: "Who will be teaching LIB classes? Is the MLS the terminal degree?"

Library's response: "Librarians at Randall Library will teach all LIB classes. All UNCW Librarians are faculty (same status as all other faculty on campus). The master's degree is the terminal degree for librarians. The American Library Association is the accrediting body for library professionals. According to ALA policy 54.2, 'The master's degree from a program accredited by the American Library Association (or from a master's level program in library and information studies accredited or recognized by the appropriate national body of another country) is the appropriate professional degree for librarians.'

(http://www.ala.org/ala/accreditation/accredfaq/faq.htm#q4). Typically, the Ph.D. in library science is earned by individuals who plan to become professors at graduate schools of library and information science, or to direct large research libraries."

Question posed by curriculum committee: "Don't academic departments already offer a research methods course?"

Library's response: "The library will not be duplicating any departmental research methods courses. The LIB 103 course is about finding, accessing, and evaluating information. The class will give students the skills to use online catalogs, electronic databases, print indexes, and major reference sources."

Question posed by curriculum committee: "How will you determine which classes to teach?"

Library's response: "The library currently collaborates with all departments to offer library instruction. We would continue to collaborate with departments to create classes if we feel there is an appropriate audience for them. We would not develop a course without consulting other departments and would also be completely open to team teaching these classes. All course proposals would go through the Library Curriculum Committee as well as all other appropriate campus committees."

Question posed by curriculum committee: "How many classes will you teach?"

Library's response: "The Library Curriculum Committee will address this issue. The library is not looking to offer a major in library science. The American Library Association (our accrediting body) holds strict guidelines for colleges and universities for library education. Schools offering any library degree are typically schools with a 'library school' and these degrees are at the master's level. We do not wish, nor are we equipped, to offer any major or minor degree in library science. The following is a list of ALA accredited schools and universities: http://www.ala.org/ala/accreditation/lisdirb/lisdirectory.htm"

Question posed by curriculum committee: "Do we want students to pay for a service?"

Library's response: "The library has always been, and will continue to be, a service organization. We continue to expand our services to our patrons. Instruction is one of the many services we provide. We offer course-related instruction, drop-in clinics, one-on-one sessions, etc. We view offering the current UNI 103 class as an expanded class with a new prefix as an additional service. Students should be able to have the option to take a course which directly impacts all of their research during their college career (both undergraduate and graduate). We are not able to teach someone the entire research process during a 15 minute conversation at the reference desk. Students should have an optional course that enables them to fully understand the research process. We will continue to be a service department offering service and instructional support to departments to support their majors, minors, and research needs."

Question posed by curriculum committee: "Would you offer a LIB 101 (1 hour) and LIB 103 (3 hour) class? Some students might find it difficult to fit a three hour class into their schedule."

Library's response: "The Library Curriculum Committee will address this suggestion. We intend to offer both options. Currently we are planning to offer LIB 103 as one of the required courses for the IT minor from Computer Science."

Question posed by curriculum committee: "Will you propose the LIB 103 class be included in the basic studies curriculum?"

Library's response: "One of the library's goals has always been to promote information literacy at UNCW. We want to integrate information literacy into the UNCW curriculum. There is no requirement on this campus for information literacy. Through our current instruction classes, our reference desk interactions, and one-on-one instruction with students, our goal is to promote information literacy. Ultimately we would encourage the university to adopt an information literacy component, but just like the computer literacy competency, there are a variety of ways academic departments can achieve it. Right now, we are asking for the prefix only and to be able to teach LIB 103."

Question posed by curriculum committee: "If you have a basic studies course, how will you accommodate all the students who would register for classes?"

Library's response: "If and when the library was to offer a basic studies course, we would be able (at a minimum) to offer 8 sections (1 section taught by each librarian on the instruction team) comprised of 25 students each (200 students each semester). We would also be able to utilize E-learning tools (such as online courses, tutorials, etc.) to offer the class to additional students. We would also partner with other departments to offer classes through team teaching and training."

Question posed by curriculum committee: "Do you have enough for a three hour credit course?"

Library's response: "Yes. The content will more than fill three credit hours. Two of our peer institutions offer similar classes (Murray State University and University of North Florida)."

After all curriculum committee questions were answered, the members of the committee approved both the proposed prefix and the three credit hour course. In order to finalize the process, the University Faculty Senate was required to approve both the prefix and the course. Fortunately, both were approved with minimal discussion and the library was permitted to offer LIB 103 in the fall of 2005. One of the current "UNI" courses was dropped and the other course ("The Electronic Library") was renamed "LIB 101: Introduction to Information Literacy" and would also be offered in the fall of 2005.

The final course name and catalog description for LIB 103 is as follows:

> **LIB 103. Introduction to Library Research and Technology (3)** Exploration of research concepts in library science and information technology with an emphasis on the evolution of information, trends and issues in using online catalogues, subscription databases, evaluating and citing online material, and using web sites for research.

Planning and development of LIB 103 by the Library Curriculum Committee took place throughout the spring and summer of 2005. The committee was comprised of four librarians: the Education Librarian, the Coordinator of Research Services (who had been teaching UNI 103 the past two semesters), the Associate University Librarian for Public Services, and the Instructional Services Coordinator who chaired the Committee. It was decided that one section of the LIB 103 course would be offered in the fall of 2005. The class size would be limited to 20 students and it would be taught in the library's instructional services room. This would provide each student with access to a desktop computer during class for hands-on activities.

COURSE OBJECTIVES AND CONTENT DEVELOPMENT FOR LIB 103

Once the course logistics were in place, the Instructional Services Coordinator, with assistance from the Library Curriculum Committee, began creating and developing a three credit hour course from scratch. The course would fulfill the needs of the information technology minor as well as provide materials and activities that would enable students to develop information literacy skills. Committee members looked for peer institutions and other institutions offering similar courses and reviewed library literature for recommendations. After several months of research and discussion, the Instructional Services Coordinator developed a draft syllabus based on a combination of a course she had previously taught in the UNCW Honors program, the UNI 103 course, and course syllabi mined from other libraries' websites. The learning objectives for the course were as follows:

- To understand the various definitions of information

- To understand the historical developments of information technologies over time

- To understand how libraries use technology for information organization, storage, access, and retrieval

- To gain interdisciplinary proficiency in seeking information via electronic subscription services and library catalogs

- To recognize the difference between the World Wide Web, library catalogs, and subscription services available via the Internet

- To gain proficiency in seeking information via the World Wide Web

- To critically evaluate World Wide Web information

- To become knowledgeable about information-related issues facing libraries and higher education

Learning objectives would be met by a combination of lectures, activities, class participation, tests, readings, and projects. A current and complete syllabus can be viewed online: http://library.uncwil.edu/web/instruction/lib103/index.html

MARKETING LIB 103

During the spring and summer of 2005, promotional flyers were created to advertise the new course as well as promote the revised LIB 101. Flyers were sent to faculty in the Department of Computer Science, the University College, and faculty in the Watson School of Education. Flyers were posted in various buildings on campus and throughout the library; they were also placed on tables where students could pick them up. The LIB courses were also highlighted on the library's homepage. In the fall of 2005, LIB 103 was filled with 20 students.

ENROLLMENT RESULTS FOR LIB 103

Challenges also came along with the successes of LIB 103. Attendance in the course was encouraging, grades for fall 2005 were high with the majority of students earning A's and B's, but there were moments of struggle. Developing course content from scratch during an already busy semester was difficult for the librarian instructor. With no financial incentive or compensation for creating and teaching the course, the instructor had to be especially dedicated to and motivated by the concept of information literacy. Additional challenges became apparent when an anonymous poll of 16 students enrolled in the class revealed students' real motivations for taking LIB 103. While some expressed an interest in learning more about library research, many stated that they signed up for the class because they hoped it "would be easy" and because "it fit into their schedule." These responses indicated that the dedication on the part of the instructor did not necessarily equate to interest or motivation on the part of students. Only half the students were aware of the information technology minor at UNCW. The declared majors and class standing of the students in the class was greatly varied. It was difficult to determine what level of research skill students had achieved or what library instruction they had previously received.

Because the initial course offering was filled, it was decided that the library would offer an additional section the following semester. In the spring of 2006, two sections of the course were offered and the same promotional strategy was used to advertise the classes. Surprisingly, both sections were filled to capacity. The Instructional Services Coordinator taught both sections of LIB 103.

One of the biggest challenges in improving the course content has been adjusting the level of readings to match a 100 level course. There are few readings about libraries or information science that were created for an undergraduate level student. Readings from "library school" programs have not been suitable. Students commented on the length and level of readings and asked for readings that were more "on their level." Finding relevant and interesting readings remains one of the biggest challenges in developing LIB 103.

Overall, the experience of establishing the "LIB" prefix and creating LIB 103 has been positive and rewarding. Plans for other librarians to teach additional sections of this course are underway and we hope to create additional courses (e.g. "Research in the Sciences;" "Research in Business," etc.). Due to the success and interest in LIB 103 and the plan for additional courses, the library is currently working on allocating an additional physical space to accommodate an ever-growing instruction program. Long range planning for a true information literacy program is only beginning to be considered at Randall Library and the creation of LIB 103 is an initial phase. UNCW is currently revising its basic studies curriculum and there is potential for inclusion of the LIB courses as a basic studies requirement at some point.

Training College Students in Information Literacy

The experience of developing an information literacy course has provided librarians at UNCW with many opportunities and positive outcomes. Surprisingly, offering LIB courses seemed to help bring additional attention to the instruction program at Randall Library and in turn increase the number of traditional instruction sessions offered. Because of the overwhelmingly positive response, librarians are eager to share the experience with other academic librarians in hopes that they too will embark on the path towards developing academic courses that will promote information literacy.

Helpful Resources:

Adams, Mignon S., and Jacquelyn M. Morris. 1985. *Teaching Library Skills for Academic Credit* Phoenix: Oryx Press.

Alexander, Linda B. 1994. LIBS 1000: A Credit Course in Library Skills at East Carolina University: ERIC.

Bernnard, Deborah F. and Trudi E. Jacobson. 2001. The Committee that Worked: Developing an Information Literacy Course by Group Process. *Research Strategies* 18 (2):133-142.

Buchanan, Lori E., DeAnne L. Luck, and Ted C. Jones. 2002. Integrating Information Literacy into the Virtual University: A Course Model. *Library Trends* 51 (2):144.

Caravello, Patti Schifter. 2000. Library Instruction and Information Literacy for the Adult Learner: A Course and Its Lessons for Reference Work. *Reference Librarian* (69/70):259-269.

Davidson, Jeanne R. 2001. Faculty and Student Attitudes toward Credit Courses for Library Skills. *College & Research Libraries* 62 (2):155-63.

Funes, Carolyn H. 2004. An Odyssey: Palomar College Develops an Information Literacy Course. *Community & Junior College Libraries* 12 (3):61-65.

Hales, Celia, and Dianne Catlett. 1984. The Credit Course: Reaffirmation from Two University Libraries' Methodology: East Carolina University. *Research Strategies* 2 (4):162.

Jacobson, Trudi E., and Lijuan Xu. 2002. Motivating Students in Credit-based Information Literacy Courses: Theories and Practice. *portal: Libraries & the Academy* 2 (3):423-442.

Kelley, Kimberly B., Gloria J. Orr, Janice Houck, and Claudine SchWeber. 2001. Library Instruction for the Next Millennium: Two Web-based Courses to Teach Distant Students Information Literacy. *Journal of Library Administration* 32 (1/2):281-294.

Lawson, Mollie D. 2000. Reaching the Masses: Marketing a Library Instruction Course to Incoming Freshmen. *Research Strategies* 17 (1):45-49.

Lindsay, Elizabeth Blakesley. 2004. Distance Teaching: Comparing Two Online Information Literacy Courses. *Journal of Academic Librarianship* 30 (6):482-487.

Manuel, Kate. 2001. Teaching an Online Information Literacy Course. *Reference Services Review* 29 (3):219-228.

Miller, Jolene Michelle. 2004. Issues Surrounding the Administration of a Credit Course for Medical Students: Survey of US Academic Health Sciences Librarians. *Journal of the Medical Library Association* 92 (3):354-363.

Muiherrin, Elizabeth, Kimberly B. Kelley, Diane Fishman, and Gloria J. Orr. 2004. Information Literacy and the Distant Student: One University's Experience Developing, Delivering, and Maintaining an Online, Required Information Literacy Course. *Internet Reference Services Quarterly* 9 (1/2):21-36.

Ojedokun, Ayoku A., and Edward Lumande. 2005. The Integration of Information Literacy Skills into a Credit-Earning Programme at the University of Botswana. *African Journal of Library, Archives & Information Science* 15 (2):117-124.

Reynolds, Leslie J. 2001. Model for a Web-based Information Literacy Course: Design, Conversion and Experiences. *Science & Technology Libraries* 19 (3/4):165-178.

Shirato, Linda, and Joseph Badics. 1997. Library Instruction in the 1990s: A Comparison with Trends in Two Earlier LOEX Surveys. *Research Strategies* 15 (4):223-37.

Wang, Rui. 2006. The Lasting Impact of Library Credit Course. *portal: Libraries & the Academy* 6 (1):79-92.

Samples of Other Information Literacy Courses Offered for Credit:

Arkansas State University: http://www.library.astate.edu/dept/ref/instruction.htm

Baruch College (CUNY): http://newman.baruch.cuny.edu/instruct/lib_course_des.htm

Central Michigan University (LIB 197)

Fresno City College: http://www.fresnocitycollege.edu/library/instruction.html

Glendale College: http://www.glendale.edu/library/IC/CreditCourses/CCindex.htm

Golden West College: http://gwc.info/library/instruction/instruction.htm

Iowa State University: http://www.lib.iastate.edu/cfora/generic.cfm?cat=class_prog&navid=10800&parent=2015

Murray State University: http://www.murraystate.edu/msml/syllabus.html

Pennsylvania State University: http://www.libraries.psu.edu/instruction/lst.htm

St. Petersburg College: http://www.spjc.edu/central/libonline/instruction/index.htm

San Francisco State University: http://www.library.sfsu.edu/Instruction/courses.html

Seattle Central Community College: http://dept.sccd.ctc.edu/cclib/Instruction/courses.asp

University at Albany: http://library.albany.edu/usered/classes/

University of Colorado at Boulder:
http://ucblibraries.colorado.edu/reference/credit.htm

University of North Florida: http://www.unf.edu/%7Ealderman/BLISS2/index.html

University of Oregon: http://libweb.uoregon.edu/instruct/credit.html

Wayne State College: http://academic.wsc.edu/conn_library/library_services/instruction/

Weber State University: http://library.weber.edu/il/team/policies.cfm

Western Washington University (various courses):
http://www.library.wwu.edu/ref/inst/creditcourse.shtml

ONE LIBRARY'S APPROACH TO ASSESSMENT: SOUTHEASTERN OKLAHOMA STATE UNIVERSITY

By Sharon L. Morrison & Susan S. Webb

GENERAL CHARACTERIZATION OF SOUTHEASTERN OKLAHOMA STATE

Southeastern Oklahoma State University, founded in 1909, is a small public, co-educational university in rural Oklahoma. Although historically the primary student market is Southeastern Oklahoma, the University also draws students from North Central Texas. In the fall of 2005, the University had a total of 4,075 undergraduate and graduate students; many of these students were the first members of their families to attend college. The students are primarily products of small towns and rural communities in Oklahoma and Texas, and enter Southeastern with varying degrees of library experience and with little or no exposure to library orientation and instruction.

NEW INFORMATION LITERACY INITIATIVES DRIVEN BY ACCREDITATION RECCOMENDATION

Traditionally, the library used general survey assessment tools and collected statistical information and collapsed them into an annual report. The report presented tallies of circulation statistics, money spent, additions and deletions to the collection, reference questions asked and answered, and library instruction sessions given. The end result was a collection of statistics, but little or no attention was given to the user's point of view. After an accreditation visit from the Higher Learning Commission in the fall of 2003, the library was charged by the University with "developing processes or a process for establishing goals and assessing progress that parallels the existing assessment plan for student learner outcomes." Recognizing the challenge of meeting the institutional goal for the library by 2007, a decision was made to expand the normal practice of relying solely on library inputs and outputs to include the user's perspective and student learner outcomes. This change constituted a paradigm shift in the library's focus and prompted the adoption of the ACRL *Standards for Libraries in Higher Education*.

A MISSION STATEMENT FOR THE LIBRARY'S INFORMATION LITERACY EFFORTS

At the onset of this change, the library determined that information literacy instruction was of cardinal importance for students to be successful. Therefore, the first priority was to determine what skills would be emphasized and formally taught. These skills were incorporated into a new mission statement which also mirrored the University's mission statement. After the statement was written, the library utilized a matrix to develop objectives and designate assessment criteria that accurately reflected patrons' needs. The assessment matrix allowed the library to see the goals, objectives and evaluative instruments in a precise, orderly way. Priorities were then written for each goal and objective. Of the fifteen established goals, ten measured inputs and outputs, two were written for student learner outcomes and three were written to address library orientation and instruction. This paper will discuss the information literacy program that is currently in place and the assessment tools used to yield valuable insights.

ASSESSMENT

The University offers a two-hour credit course called *College Success* or *First Year Experience*. The class is recommended for all incoming freshmen; however, it is a requirement for any student enrolled in remedial courses, any student with an ACT score of 19 or below, and any student with an undecided major. The University has found a direct positive correlation between the student retention rate and the completion rate in the College Success class by first term freshmen students. Additional evidence-based assessment by the University indicates that upon completion of this class, students' basic and research skills dramatically increased. Prior to the fall of 2005, the library had never formally assessed students' progress either in basic library skills or in information literacy skills. Because of this, the library added an assessment tool to evaluate data-supported progress in information literacy and basic library instruction.

The library participates in the *College Success* class by providing five days of information literacy instruction designed to introduce the student to basic resources. The goals are to enable the student to become more information literate and an independent user of the library. During these five days the librarians teach information literacy and critical thinking and information retrieval skills. The library first gives a virtual tour of the library's web page and this tour introduces the student to basic library information and important links. One resource covered and assigned as homework is *Searchpath*, an online library tutorial. .The *Searchpath* software is in the public domain and therefore can be adapted to a specific library program. Because it is comprehensive and online, *Searchpath* fulfills the general education requirements of the class, *Computers in Society*.

Training College Students in Information Literacy

A twenty-five question *Information Literacy Quiz* is given on the first day as a pre-test of the students overall library knowledge. On days two through five, the library introduces electronic resources: *Sirsi*, (the on-line catalog), *Academic Search Elite*, (an on-line general magazine/journal database), *Occupational Outlook Handbook* and *Statistical Abstracts* (on-line government documents). Each resource was carefully chosen for its broad, representational scope. These on-line resources provide students the opportunity to learn how to develop search terms and concepts, search using the concepts, ascertain if the results are relevant and retrieve the information. Instructors emphasize transference of this skill from database to database and for homework students receive a worksheet covering each electronic resource. The *Information Literacy Quiz* is given the final day and used as a post-test assessment.

The study resulted in far more data than can be thoroughly described here but some overall findings can be presented. Prior to the implementation of quantitative assessment tools, the library module for *College Success* had been informally analyzed for its relevance to the primary course objectives by the librarians who teach the course, and then adjusted accordingly. With the new evaluative tools the librarians were able to obtain specific information and target problem areas. For example, the students enrolled in the *College Success* classes who completed both the pre- and post tests had an improvement of 11.63%. Overall, however, it also indicated that of the 358 students enrolled, only 143 actually completed the information literacy pre- and post- tests. Further examination determined which questions gave students the most trouble, giving librarians important knowledge for decision making. The problem areas were then targeted for the next semester.

One hundred ninety four (194) of the 358 students enrolled completed the homework assignment *in Searchpath*, the on-line tutorial. The students having this framework of information prior to library instruction correspondingly scored higher on the Information Literacy pre- and post-tests. Students that completed *Searchpath* and the Information Literacy quiz also received significantly higher scores on the final worksheet.

For the basic "one-shot" bibliographic instruction, the library designed an on-line survey for library instruction, which is qualitative and includes a section for student comments. Students take this survey at the end of the session and results are delivered directly into an *Access* database. At the end of the semester results are tabulated and analyzed. From this information, the library ascertained what program changes, if any, needed to be made.

The library at Southeastern Oklahoma State University continually assesses its information literacy efforts. The charge from the Higher Learning Commission has served as the catalyst to formally make changes to reassess our mission and evaluate how the library fulfills that mission. Use of the ACRL *Standards for Libraries in Higher Education* has been beneficial to the library by encouraging focus on assessment processes. The result has been empirical data utilized for effective and responsive changes and future planning.

INFORMATION LITERACY INITIATIVES AT CENTRAL CONNECTICUT STATE UNIVERSITY

By Susan Slaga

COLLEGE DESCRIPTION

Central Connecticut State University (CCSU) is the oldest public institution of higher education in Connecticut. It is located about ten miles west of Hartford in New Britain, CT. In the fall of 2005, the university enrolled 12,315 students (graduate and undergraduate); 7, 976 are full-time. Close to 5,000 students are enrolled in the School of Arts and Sciences and slightly over 3,000 in the School of Education and Professional Studies. CCSU also has over 3,000 students enrolled in the Schools of Business and Technology.

STAFF AND CLASSES

Elihu Burritt Library at CCSU has a staff of 47 employees. Classes are taught by seven of the reference librarians on staff. Two of the reference librarians teach the majority of the classes while the others teach as needed or when requested.

In 2005, CCSU's Buritt Library offered 268 information literacy classes (serving almost 6, 000 students) and the number continues to grow. Ten years ago, the library gave fewer than 195 classes to roughly 3, 900 students. Classes typically involve an orientation for freshman students and include a tour, but many are subject specific-sessions in such fields as education, psychology, or business. Most classes last about an hour.

Burritt Library also offers a semester long one credit class called *Library Resources and Skills*. Three sections are offered during the fall and spring semesters, one of which is offered online to distance students through WebCT. The class, an elective, fulfills the general education requirement.

The class meets once a week and usually includes a lecture, in-class assignments and a little time to start homework. For the first class, a tour of the library is given along with an overview of the course and the library's website. During the rest of the semester the following subjects are usually taught: searching the online catalog at an advanced level; learning the parts of bibliographic citations and how and why to use them; understanding call numbers and the Library of Congress classification system; searching multidisciplinary and subject specific databases at an advanced level; using different search engines to search the World Wide Web;

evaluating websites; and plagiarism. One instructor has also added a unit about RSS feeds and how to set them up. He also teaches this unit as a workshop for faculty.

ASSESSMENT

Assessment for this class is done through weekly homework assignments and a mid-term and final exam and/or assignment. Most of the students do very well, earning high grades of A's and B's. Additionally, course evaluations are distributed at the end of the semester and most students are very satisfied with the class and instructors and find it very useful. Many of the seniors who complete the class wish they had taken it when they were freshman because it was so helpful. Burritt Library would like offer more sections of this class in the future if more staff can be hired.

COMBINING 1-CREDIT INFORMATION LITERACY CLASSES WITH ENGLISH, PSYCHOLOGY & HISTORY 3-CREDIT CLASSES

The reference staff at Burritt Library will be writing a proposal to offer a section of *Library Resources and Skills* for CCSU's Learning Communities initiative for 2007. A pilot program for this initiative will start in fall 2006 during which several freshmen will be enrolled in some interdisciplinary classes. They will be either team taught and share the same texts and/or reading materials, or have an extra credit added to a three credit class, and encompass a study skills or information literacy component. The librarians believe that combining our one credit class with English, Psychology, History or other classes will be very beneficial to students.

On a smaller scale, Burrittt Library is already conducting its own similar pilot program during the spring 2006 semester. A reference librarian and history professor have teamed up to teach *The Historical Imagination*, a research class. This class is required for all history majors at CCSU and the subject matter for the class varies each semester depending on the instructor. The class is focusing on the Richard Loeb and Nathan Leopold murder trial case in Chicago, Illinois in 1924 and other important topics from that time period such as the death penalty, anti-Semitism, urban Chicago, etc. It is a very intense class with extensive reading and writing assignments, book reviews, research outlines, annotated bibliographies, and a large research paper at the end of the semester.

The staff noticed a need for more instruction for this particular class. The typical "one shot" lecture instruction session in the beginning of the semester was not enough. After just one session, several students were still not sure how to properly use the library's databases or could not distinguish between a primary and secondary source.

We learned about an embedded librarian program at Daniel Webster College in Nashua, NH, where the public services librarian team taught a freshman composition class with an English professor. This enabled the students to learn course content and enhance their research and writing skills at the same time. After reading more on the subject and meeting with the faculty who initiated the program at Daniel Webster College, we decided to try a similar type of program at CCSU.

Instead of one library instruction session taught at the beginning of the semester, three sessions would be taught throughout the semester as students worked on different assignments. To reinforce the topics presented, students would also be asked questions during the lecture and given graded library homework assignments. The students seem very eager so far and usually take notes and ask questions during the instruction sessions. Most students also did well on their first library assignment, which indicates that many of them are retaining what they've been taught. The students are also required to hold at least one individual consultation with a librarian during the course of the semester. This will allow them to ask questions about their research and use of library resources and to make sure they are on the right track with their research papers.

To assess what the students have learned, they were given a short answer pre-test at the beginning of the semester, and they will be given the same test at the end of the semester. Their progress with the homework assignments will also be examined throughout the semester.

ONLINE TUTORIALS AND REACHING DISTANCE STUDENTS

Last semester reference librarians developed several online tutorials for our distance students and off campus users. Since a good number of CCSU's students are part-time commuters, we thought this would be beneficial, since many of them can't get to campus for information literacy instruction or to ask questions. We also have many students who are new to using our library (such as freshmen or older adults returning to school, etc.). We decided to make some basic tutorials first and, as time allows, we plan to make some subject specific tutorials. Since we had never created our own tutorials, we received a lot assistance and support from CCSU's Media Center. They recommended and supplied *Captivate* software for the tutorials. It is very user-friendly and allows you to create your own mini "movies" that will be used as tutorials. It records your application (video, moving screenshots, etc.) You can edit, add captions, videos, hyperlinks, rollovers, etc.). This software is more geared toward educational use. It also allows you to interact with your users if you choose. You can also email the movies, publish them online or on a CD-ROM, etc.

After the tutorials' text and instructions were written, they were completed and posted on the library's website (http://library.ccsu.edu/). Three tutorials show how to search the online catalog (author, title and keyword). One demonstrates how to electronically request a book from any other Connecticut State University.. Also there are tutorials that show students how to order books and articles through interlibrary loan; how to access journal articles and other materials that are available through electronic reserves; how to log on from off campus and access the library's databases, and how to search for articles using the *Academic Search*

Premier database. The students and faculty who have used the tutorials have found them to be very valuable and beneficial. They occupy a prominent place on our new website and are also promoted in many of our classes and individual sessions as well as campus listservs.

Burritt Library is also in the process of updating and creating new research/resource guides. To date, the library has completed guides on how to use the EBSCO and Proquest databases as well as psychology, sociology and music resources.

Another way we reach our distance learners is through the online version of the Library Resources and Skills class that is offered once a year. It is very similar in content to our onsite version discussed earlier. The class "meets" online once a week. Most of the students are from CCSU, but sometimes they are from the other state universities or even other countries. Students access the course through Central Pipeline, CCSU's online campus portal. The reference librarian uses WebCT to post lecture notes, information, grades, and assignments. Participants meet each week in a chat area for a discussion and students also have chat area-discussions among themselves.

ADVICE FOR PEERS

Find out what students need to learn to be more successful with their research. Based on those findings, come up with new ideas on how to reach students and better instruct them. It also helps to promote the library and its services and resources to faculty and the administration as well, in order to gain more support for new programs and ideas. The library's instructional programs should fulfill the larger institutional mission to educate and help students be successful at school and in life.

OTHER REPORTS FROM PRIMARY RESEARCH GROUP

PREVAILING & BEST PRACTICES IN ELECTRONIC AND PRINT SERIALS MANAGEMENT
Price: $80.00   Publication Date: November 2005   ISBN: 1-57440-076-2

This report looks closely at the electronic and print serials procurement and management practices of eleven libraries including: The University of Ohio, Villanova University; the Colorado School of Mines, Carleton College, Northwestern University; Baylor University, Princeton University, the University of Pennsylvania, the University of San Francisco, Embry-Riddle Aeronautical University and the University of Nebraska Medical Center. The report looks at both electronic and print serials and includes discussions of the following issues: selection and management of serials agents, including the negotiation of payment; allocating the serials budget by department; resolving access issues with publishers; use of consortiums in journal licensing; invoice reconciliation and payment; periodicals binding, claims, check in and management; serials department staff size and range of responsibilities; serials management software; use of open access archives and university depositories; policies on gift subscriptions, free trials and academic exchanges of publications; use of electronic serials/catalog linking technology; acquisition of usage statistics; cooperative arrangements with other local libraries and other issues in serials management.

CREATING THE DIGITAL ART LIBRARY
Price: $80.00   Publication Date: October 2005   ISBN: 1-57440-074-6

This special report looks at the efforts of ten leading art libraries and image collections to digitize their holdings. The study reports on the efforts of The National Gallery of Canada, Cornell University's Knight Resource Center, the University of North Carolina, Chapel Hill; the Smithsonian Institution Libraries, The Illinois Institute of Technology, The National Archives and Records Administration, McGill University, Ohio State University, the Cleveland Museum of Art, and the joint effort of Harvard, Princeton, The University of California, San Diego, the University of Minnesota and others to develop a union catalog for cultural objects.

Among the issues covered: cost of outsourcing, cost of in-house conversions, the future of 35 mm slides and related equipment, use of ARTstor and other commercial services, ease of interlibrary loan in images and the creation of a union catalog, prioritizing holdings for digitization, relationship of art libraries to departmental image collections, marketing image collections, range of end users of image collections, determining levels of access to the collection, digitization and distribution of backup materials on artists lives and times, equipment selection, copyright, and other issues in the creation and maintenance of digital art libraries.

TRENDS IN THE MANAGEMENT OF LIBRARY SPECIAL COLLECTIONS IN FILM AND PHOTOGRAPHY
Price: $80.00   Publication Date: October 2005   ISBN: 1-57440-075-4

This special report looks at the management and development of America's thriving special collections in film and photography. The report profiles the following collections: The University of Louisville, the Photographic Archives; the University of Utah's Multimedia Collection; The American Institute of Physics' Emilio Segre Visual Archives; The Newsfilm Library at the University of South Carolina; The University of California, Berkeley Pacific Film Archive; the UCLA Film and Television Archive, the Vanderbilt University Television News Archive; The National Archives and Records Administration's Special Media Preservation Laboratory; the University of Washington's Digital Initiatives.

The report covers digitization of photographs and film, special collection marketing, collection procurement, funding and financing, approaches for optimizing both sales revenues and educational uses, development of web-based sale and distribution systems for photography and film, systems to assure copyright compliance, the development of online searchable databases, and many other aspects of film and photography special collection management.

EMERGING BEST PRACTICES IN LEGAL RECORDS MANAGEMENT
Publication Date: March 2006   Price: $295.00

This special report is based on detailed interviews with records managers, practice management directors and partners in major law firms and other legal offices. Among the organizational participants are: Kaye Scholer, Fulbright & Jawarski, Kilpatrick Stockton, Thomas Cooley Law School , the National Archives & Records Administration, Thompson Hine, Dewey Ballantine and Blackwell Sanders Peper Martin.

Among the issues covered in detail: Records Department Staff Size, Budget & Range of Responsibilities, Breakdown of Employee Time Use, Space Benchmarks for Off-site storage, Classification Scheme and Planning for Records Retrieval, Integration of Records with Copyright Information, Emails, Correspondence and other Forms of Legal Information, Types of Knowledge Management Software/Systems Under Consideration, Uses of Records Request Tracking, Strategies for Employee and Attorney Training in Content Control, Use of RFID & Barcoding Technology, Pace & Cost of Records Digitization, Digitization Technology & Storage Options, Records Security & Password Strategy, Relations Among the Library, Docket, Records Department, Information Technology Department and other Units Involved in Content/Knowledge Management and much more.

MAXIMIZING LAW LIBRARY PRODUCTIVITY
ISBN: 1-57440-077-0   PRICE: $89.50   Publication Date: March 2006

This report looks closely at a broad range of management practices of law firm libraries including those from the following institutions: Foley & Hoag; Northwestern Mutual Insurance; Nelson, Mullins Riley And Scarborough; Cornell University Law School; Schwabe Williamson & Wyatt; Mayer, Brown, Rowe & Maw; Loyola University Law School; Sonnenschein Nath & Rosenthal; Brinks, Hofer, Gilson & Lione; The Civil Court of the City of New York; Beuf Gilbert and others.

The many issues covered include: trends in the physical space allocated to the library, print vs. electronic information spending, retention policies on print reporters, uses of blogs, personnel and training policies, outsourcing, relations with records and knowledge/content management, ways to serve multiple offices and locations, use of RSS feeds and weblogs, uses of intranets and other shared workspaces, information literacy training, favored databases, optimizing librarian time management, management of the flow of reference requests, software selection and other issues impacting the performance of law libraries.

LAW LIBRARY BENCHMARKS, 2004-05 EDITION
Publication Date: August 20004
Price: $115.00   ISBN #:   1-57440-070-3

Law Library Benchmarks presents data from more than 70 law libraries, including those of major law firms, law schools, government agencies and courthouses. Data is broken out by type of law library. Includes detailed data on: library dimensions and physical and "e-traffic" to the library, trends in library staff size, salaries and budget, precise statistics on use of librarian time, spending trends in the library content budget, spending on specific types of legal information such as state and local codes or legal journals, spending on databases and commercial online services, use of and plans for CD-ROM, parent organization management's view of the future of the law library, assessment of library resources for analyzing the business side of law, assessment of attorney search skills, trends in use of reference materials and much more.

CREATING THE DIGITAL LAW LIBRARY
Price: $95.00 Publication Date: June 1   2003

This report profiles digital library development policies of leading law libraries including those of Thompson Hine, Cassells Brock & Blackwell, Seyfarth Shaw, Ivins Phillips & Barker, Querrey @ Harrow, Lawrence County Law Library, Duke University Law Library, the University of Indiana Law Library, and others.   The report covers policies concerning electronic journals, archiving, e-books, electronic directories, database user training, use of alert service, virtual reference services, negotiating tactics with vendors, electronic documents delivery, librarian time management, web site redevelopment and design and other issues.

BEST PRACTICES OF ACADEMIC LIBRARY INFORMATION TECHNOLOGY DIRECTORS
Price: $75.00   Publication Date: February 25, 2005   ISBN: 1-57440-072-X

This study is based on interviews with IT directors and assistant directors of leading college and university libraries and consortiums, including The Research Libraries Group, Vanderbilt University, the University of Texas, Lewis & Clark College, Salt Lake Community College, the University of Washington, the California Institute of Technology, Hutchinson Community College and Australia's Monash University,

Among the many topics covered are: investment in and maintenance of workstations, implementation of wireless access, policies towards laptops in the library, digitizing special collections, establishing digital depositories, preserving scholarly access to potentially temporal digital media, use of Ebooks, services for distance learning students, use of url resolvers, web site development and management, use of virtual reference, investment in library software, IT staff size and staff skill composition, range of IT staff responsibilities, use of outsourcing, relations between Library and general University IT staff, uses of PHP programming, catalog integration with the web, catalog enhancement software and services, web site search engine policies, use of automated electronic collection management software, technology education and training, development of technology centers and information literacy, library printing technology and cost reimbursement, and other issues of concern to library information technology staff directors.

THE MARKETING OF HISTORIC SITES, MUSEUMS, EXHIBITS AND ARCHIVES
Price: $95.00   Publication Date: JUNE 2005   ISBN: 1-57440-056-8

This report looks closely at how history is presented and marketed by organizations such as history museums, libraries, historical societies, and historic sites and monuments. The report profiles the efforts of The Vermont Historical Society, Hook's Historic Drug Store and Pharmacy, The Thomas Jefferson Foundation/Monticello, the Musee Conti Wax Museum of New Orleans, The Bostonian Society, the Dittrick Medical History Center, The Band Museum, the Belmont Mansion, the Kansas State Historical Society, the Computer History Museum, the Atari Virtual Museum, the Museum of American Financial History, the Atlanta History Center and the public libraries of Denver and Evansville. The Study's revealing profiles, based on extensive interviews with executive directors and marketing managers of the institutions cited, provide a deeply detailed look at how history museums, sites, societies and monuments are marketing themselves.

BEST PRACTICES OF PUBLIC LIBRARY INFORMATION TECHNOLOGY DIRECTORS
Price: $65.00   FEBRUARY 2005   ISBN: 1-57440-073-8

This special report from Primary Research Group is based on exhaustive interviews with information technology directors and other critical staff involved in IT decision-making from the Princeton Public Library, the Minneapolis Public Library, the Boston Public Library, the Seattle Public Library, Cedar Rapids Public Library, San Francisco Public Library, the Denver Public Library, Evansville Public Library and the Santa Monica Public Library. The report – which is in an interview format and presents the views of the institutions cited above as well as Primary Research Group commentary – presents insights into the myriad of technology-related issues confronting today's public librarians, including issues involved with: internet filtering, workstation management and development, PC image roll out, equipment and vendor selection, database licensing, internet-access policies, automated book check-in and check-out systems, cataloging, and catalog enhancement, voice over IP, digitization of special collections, development of technology centers, wireless access, use of e-books, outsourcing, IT-staff training, virtual reference, and much more.

TRAINING COLLEGE STUDENTS IN INFORMATION LITERACY: PROFILES OF HOW COLLEGES TEACH THEIR STUDENTS TO USE ACADEMIC LIBRARIES
PRICE: $69.50   JANUARY   2003   ISBN: 1-57440-059-2

This special report profiles how more than a dozen academic libraries are coping with the surge of web/database education requests. The report covers the development of online tutorials, distribution of teaching loads and levels of specialization among library staff, the perils of teaching library science to English 101 and Psychology 101 students, as well as advanced personalized tutorials for PhD candidates and professors. Among the specialized topics covered: How libraries are reaching out and teaching distance learners and how are they negotiating help from other college departments, such as academic computing and education, and from in-house instructional technology programmers. Other issues explored include the library-education efforts of consortiums and partnerships, use of knowledge-management and reference software for library training, the development of savvy library web pages and tutorials for training, and the thorny issue of negotiating training support from vendors.

CREATING THE VIRTUAL REFERENCE SERVICE
PRICE: $85.00   JANUARY 2003
ISBN: 1-57440-058-4

This report profiles the efforts of 15 academic, special, and public libraries to develop digital reference services. The aim of the study is to enable other libraries to benefit from their experience in deciding whether, and how, to develop a digital-reference service, how much time, money and other resources to spend on it, how to plan it, institute it and evaluate it. Let librarians – in their own words – tell you about their experiences with digital reference.

Among the libraries and other organizations profiled are: Pennsylvania State University, Syracuse University's Virtual Reference Desk, the Massachusetts Institute of Technology, Palomar College, The Library of Congress, the University of Florida, PA Librarian Live, the Douglas County Public Library, the Cleveland Public Library, Denver Public Library, OCLC, the New England Law Library Consortium, the Internet Public Library, Paradise Valley Community College, Yale University Law School, Oklahoma State University, Tutor.Com and Baruch College.

PRIVATE COLLEGE INFORMATION TECHNOLOGY BENCHMARKS
PRICE: $295   JANUARY 2003
ISBN: 1-57440-060-6

Private College Information Technology Benchmarks presents more than 650 tables and charts exploring the use of information technology by small- and medium-sized private colleges in the United States. The report covers both academic and administrative computing, and breaks out data by enrollment size and level of tuition charged. Sixteen private American colleges contributed data to the report.

LICENSING AND COPYRIGHT MANAGEMENT: BEST PRACTICES OF COLLEGE, SPECIAL, AND RESEARCH LIBRARIES
PRICE: $80   MAY 2004   ISBN: 1-57440-068-1

This report looks closely at the licensing and copyright-management strategies of a sample of leading research, college and special libraries and consortiums and includes interviews with leading experts. The focus is on electronic-database licensing, and includes discussions of the most pressing issues: development of consortiums and group buying initiatives, terms of access, liability for infringement, archiving, training and development, free-trial periods, contract language, contract-management software and time-management issues, acquiring and using usage statistics, elimination of duplication, enhancement of bargaining power, open-access publishing policies, interruption-of-service contingency arrangements, changes in pricing over the life of the contract, interlibrary loan of electronic files, copyright clearance, negotiating tactics, uses of consortiums, and many other issues. The report profiles the emergence of consortiums and group-buying arrangements.

CREATING THE DIGITAL ACADEMIC LIBRARY:
Price: $69.50   JULY 2004   ISBN: 1-57440- 071-1

This report looks closely at the efforts of more than ten major academic libraries to develop their digital assets and deal with problems in the area of librarian time management, database selection, vendor relations, contract negotiation and tracking, electronic-resources funding and marketing, technical development, archival access, open access publishing agit prop, use of e-books, digitization of audio and image collections and other areas of the development of the digital academic library. The report includes profiles of Columbia University School of Medicine, the Health Sciences Complex of the University of Texas, Duke University Law Library, the University of Indiana Law Library, the University of South Carolina, the University of Idaho, and many others.